Agatahi:

The Cherokee Trail of Tears

Also by W. Jeff Bishop

Newnan

Coweta County: A Brief History

A Cold Coming

Myth & History: The John Ross House through Time

Running Waters: Forgotten Cherokee Council Ground

ᎠᏕᎳᏅ: The Cherokee Trail of Tears

A People's Resistance Against the Forced Removal from their Southeast Homeland as Related in their Own Words

W. Jeff Bishop

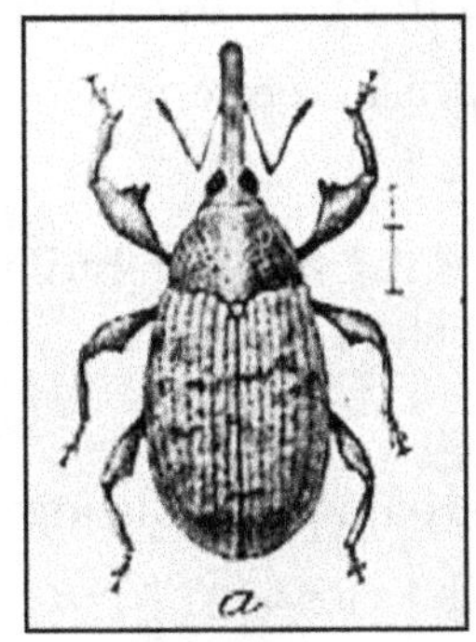

Boll Weevil Press

2017

Published by Boll Weevil Press

Boll Weevil Press

Newnan, GA

Library of Congress Cataloging-in-Publication Data

Bishop, W. Jeff, 1969-

Agatahi: The Cherokee Trail of Tears — A People's Resistance against the Forced Removal from their Southeast Homeland, as Related in their Own Words

Includes bibliographical references.

ISBN 978-0-9889568-7-2

1.Trail of Tears, 1838 2. Cherokee Indians—Relocation. 3. Cherokee Indians—History—Sources.

Cover designed by Barbara Long Bishop

Book designed by Dale Lyles

For Barbara,

and for the Cherokee people.

Contents

Acknowledgements

There are so many people to acknowledge, and always the fear that someone important will be inadvertently left out. At the top of my list are Dr. Sarah Hill and Jim Langford, who first inspired me to find out more about the Cherokee Removal, and who provided me with so many valuable experiences and sources. Also I want to thank Dr. Ann McCleary, my mentor in the field of public history. Of infinite assistance and guidance was Michael Wren, whose research dwarfs my own. I thank Dr. Vicki Rozema and Dr. Theda Perdue, whose books on the Cherokee Removal helped to inspire this one. Dr. Ben Steere's passion for Cherokee history and culture was also an inspiration. I wish to thank Jack Baker, Troy Wayne Poteete, Jerra Quinton Baker, Brett Riggs, and the entire Trail of Tears Association organization for everything they have done to tell the story of the Trail of Tears and to preserve and interpret what remains of the material culture of that era. I also want to thank the National Park Service, especially the people who work in the Santa Fe office for the Historic Trails division, including Aaron Mahr, Sharon Brown, Steve Burns, Frank Norris, Lynne Mager, and Carol S. Clark. I thank former Cherokee Chief Chad Smith and Dr. Julia Coates for the Cherokee Nation History course they put together, which served as a valuable introduction for me, providing a lens of understanding. The people involved with the Georgia chapter of the Trail of Tears Association have always been like an extended family, including Linda Baker, Leslie Thomas, Tony Harris, Linda Geiger, Linda Fletcher, Patsy Edgar, Jeff Stancil, Dola Davis, Daniel Davis, Carra Harris, Myra Reidy, J.B. Tate, Tommy Cox, Doug Mabry, Bill and Eugenia Cavender, and so many others, I want to thank Marybelle Chase of the Oklahoma chapter of the Trail of Tears Association for compiling many of the Cherokee claims against the government used in this book. I thank the Newnan-Coweta Historical Society, as well, David Gomez of the New Echota State Historic Site, and Julia Autry of the Chief Vann House.

I hope that this modest compilation will help contribute to the ongoing conversation, and provide one more way of telling this important story.

As always, I must thank my wife, Barbara, and our children (Ellory, Peyton, Hetty, Sophie, and Truman), without whom none of what I do would be possible.

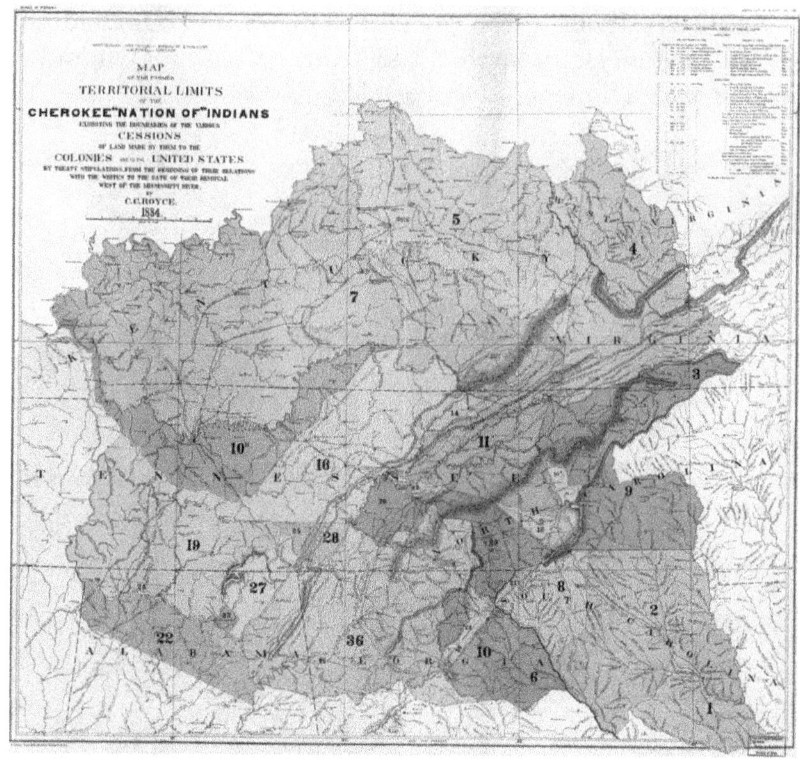

Figure 1. Cherokee land sessions as outlined by Charles C. Royce in 1884. This map shows the original claimed territorial limits of the Cherokee Nation, extending as far north as Kentucky.

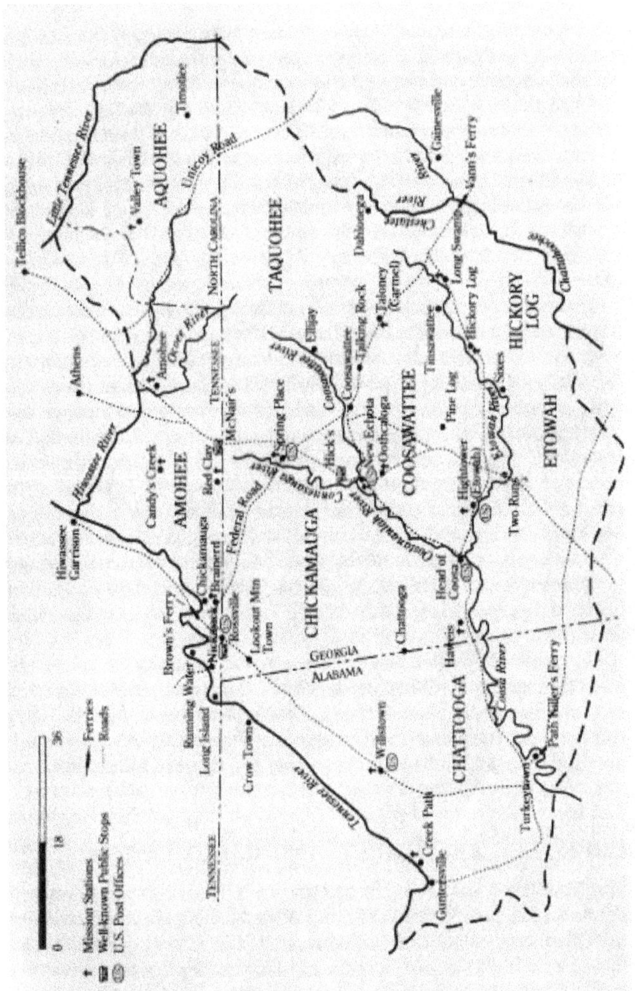

Figure 2. A map developed by Jeff Stancil showing the extent of the Cherokee Nation and its principal towns just prior to the Removal period, in the early nineteenth century. The area included Northwest Georgia, Western North Carolina, East Alabama, and Southeast Tennessee.

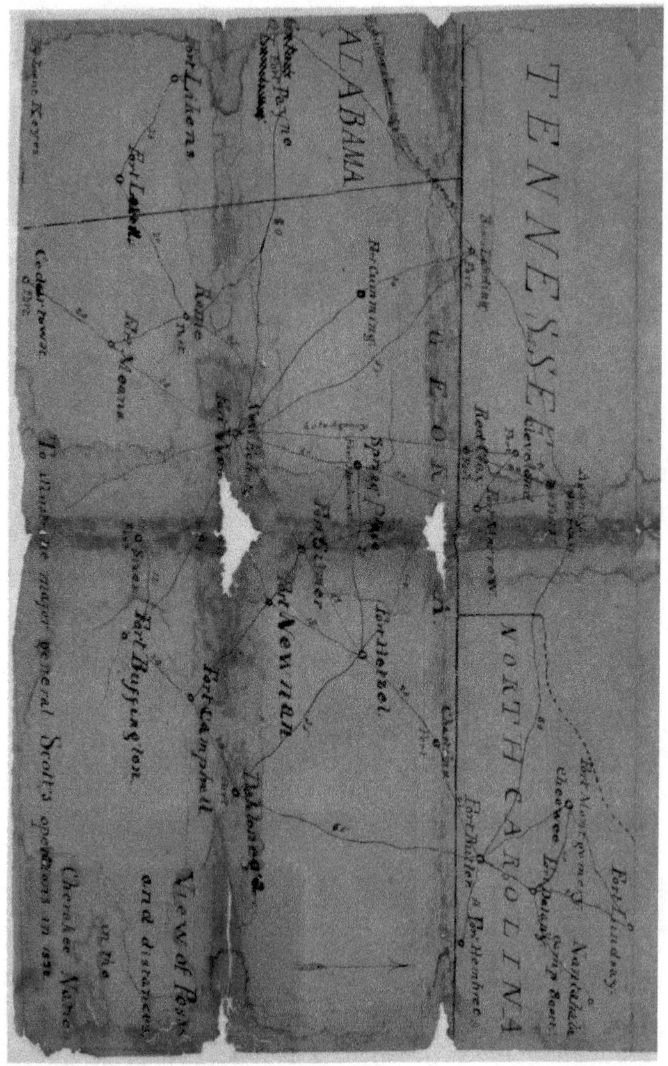

Figure 3. A map drawn during Cherokee Removal military operations, showing the various forts and camps established in the spring of 1838, and their distances from one another.

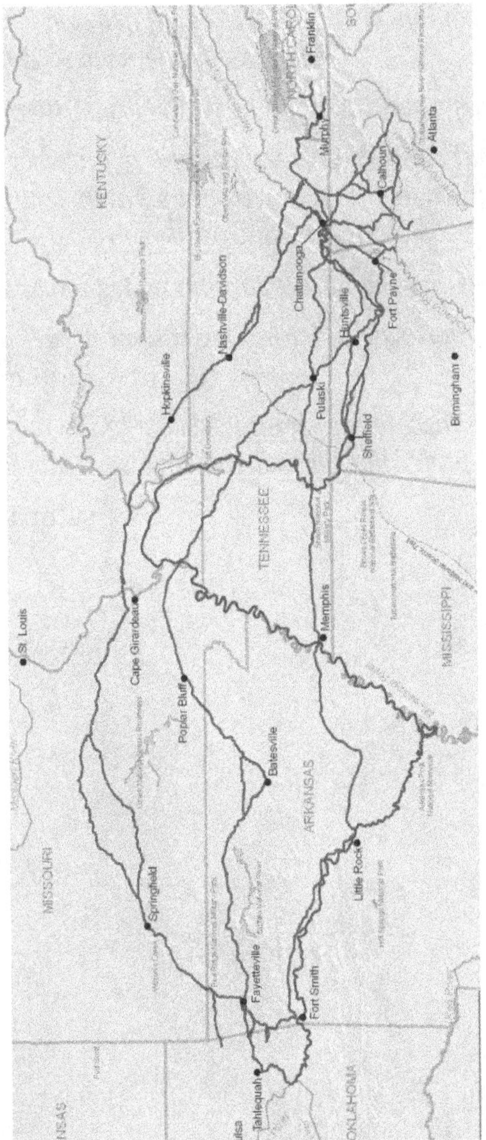

Figure 4. A basic map developed by the National Park Service and the Trail of Tears Association showing the various routes taken by the Cherokee during their removal to the West.

By the rivers of Babylon, there we sat down, yea, we wept,
when we remembered Zion.

We hanged our harps upon the willows in the midst thereof.

For there they that carried us away captive required of us
a song; and they that wasted us required of us mirth, saying,
Sing us one of the songs of Zion.

How shall we sing the Lord's song in a strange land?

If I forget thee, O Jerusalem, let my right hand forget her
cunning.

If I do not remember thee, let my tongue cleave to the roof of
my mouth; if I prefer not Jerusalem above my chief joy.

Psalm 137

Preface

Many books have been written about the so-called "Trail of Tears," the forced removal of the Cherokee people from their homeland in the American Southeast nearly 180 years ago, but they contain precious little testimony from the Cherokee people themselves. When they do include those voices, they typically are those of the political elites such as John Ross, Elias Boudinot, and John Ridge. Where are the voices of the Cherokee subsistence farmer? The widow with young children? The toll collector? The student? The orphan? This book is my humble attempt to give a fuller picture.

You will find this volume more of a curated compilation of primary sources than a "book proper." That is intentional. I thought it best to let the witnesses of this brutal era of American history speak to what they were experiencing. The most helpful thing I could do in this instance, rather than try to interpret or contextualize, would be to—as much as possible—remove myself. There will be other books, other opportunities, for interpretation. This work simply aims to restore Cherokee voices to the telling of this event we have come to call the "Trail of Tears."

Of course it was necessary, for the sake of a clear narrative, to also include the voices of important non-Indian actors in this tragedy, such as U.S. presidents George Washington, Andrew Jackson, and Martin Van Buren, and the various Georgia governors, as well as some of the important military figures involved in carrying out the operation, and witnesses who sent first-hand accounts to newspapers. White missionaries also played a key role in the recording of these events, and any account of the Trail of Tears would suffer immensely without their inclusion. But my aim, as much as possible, was to let the Cherokee people of the nineteenth century (for whom we have records) guide and shape the narrative themselves with their testimony.

I did take some (small) liberties. Readers will notice that most of the Cherokee testimony (transcribed from official claims filed against the U.S. government) is presented as first-person narrative. It wasn't always recorded that way. The claims of the Cherokees filed in 1842 were recorded in a variety of styles, at times veering wildly from first-person to third-person and back again within the same claim. For the sake of consistency (and, if I'm being honest, for simple emotional directness), I chose to present most of these claims in the first person. Academic historians wanting the precise pronouns are encouraged to go back to the original claims rather than rely on my admittedly loose transcriptions, in these instances.

In the footnotes I have included the book sources I used, along with an online source, when available, since I thought these useful for teaching purposes.

A word or two regarding problems with memorialization would seem appropriate here. What are we trying to do when we "re-member," or put back together what is lost or broken? Are we just co-opting tragic events in our history like the Trail of Tears for a kind of risk-free visceral experience? Are our attempts to make these events seem more "real" or authentic, to transform them into experiences, just a means to commodify our past, to cynically turn these things—this harrowing, real stuff experienced by real people—into something we can sell, like a t-shirt or movie, a park pass, or even this very book you hold in your hands? Are you and I guilty of being colonialists, exploiters of tragedy, all over again? Maybe we are looking to find meaning, or personal transformation, or emotional purging, or some other kind of gratification. Maybe we are attempting to control how these events are remembered. Are we trying to absolve ourselves of "white guilt," or conversely (perversely) to experience "white power" at its horrific peak? Is reading (or writing) this book a moral act or an immoral one?

I don't know.

But I do know this: if we don't feel something about history, we won't connect with it or care about it. If we don't care about history, we won't spend time thinking deeply about it and learning from it. If we don't learn from history, we will have wasted a valuable tool to shape the present and future of this increasingly anxiety-ridden world we live in.

So, yes, this book was written to provoke you: to make you feel something. Because that's the first step.

What feeling, then, am I trying to induce?

Why not read the book, and then you tell me. I think my hope is that you will feel something like what I felt when

I gathered this source material, these eyewitness accounts describing, in vivid detail, what happened here in the United States in 1838. (Or maybe you'll feel something entirely different than what I felt. That's okay, too.)

Only if you feel nothing at all will I feel like I have failed you.

And not just you.

W. Jeff Bishop

2017

Introduction: Lost Voices

The Cherokee people's forced removal from their homeland occurred in the spring of 1838 and, although much has been written in the intervening years about the so-called "Trail of Tears," the actual Cherokee experience of this traumatic and transformative event has been only sparsely studied and documented.

Although the Smithsonian produced three ethnographic studies of the Cherokee, the Removal itself earned only a passing mention. The most significant histories of Indian Removal, those by Grant Foreman and Angie Debo, were written in the 1930s and focus on all five so-called "civilized" tribes, devoting only a handful of pages to the Cherokee. A number of amateur and local historians authored books in the 1930s that focused specifically on the Cherokees, and although many made important contributions to the field and were much more expansive than the more scholarly studies of Foreman and Debo, not a single one of them made the Removal the focus of their work. More complete histories of the Cherokee were written by scholars in the mid-twentieth century, but the approaches are now outdated and, again, the Removal itself is given only passing notice. More modern approaches, focusing on gender and class, were undertaken by Theda Perdue and William G. McLoughlin in the 1980s and 1990s, but the primary focus of both historians has been on the evolution of Cherokee identity, and not on the Removal itself. The most recent contributions to the discourse, by scholars such as Tiya Miles and Tyler Boulware, also take scant notice of the Removal. In fact, for all the popular knowledge of and interest concerning the "Trail of Tears," to date there has been no book-length, scholarly treatment of the Cherokee Removal, focusing squarely on the Cherokee perspective, using readily available first-person accounts.

In the Fifth Annual Report of the Bureau of Ethnology to the Secretary of the Smithsonian Institution, in 1883-1884, ethnographer Charles C. Royce called his study the first history of the Cherokee Nation. Royce's overview, ranging from the Hernando DeSoto expedition in 1540 through the post-Civil War period, is organized primarily on a treaty-by-treaty basis, giving the Treaty of New Echota, the removal treaty, a major emphasis.[1] Royce touches on the two Supreme Court decisions that involved the Cherokee, as well as the political murders of members of the various factions of the Cherokee Nation. Royce also makes note of Chief John Ross' attempts to petition Congress, and he gives summaries of various speeches, both for and against Removal. Royce's work was part of a larger "historical atlas" of Indian affairs and land cessions, in which he intended to delineate "the boundaries of the various tracts of country which have from time to time been acquired ... from the several Indian tribes resident within the present territory of the United States from the beginning of the Federal period to the present day." These treaty summaries were to be accompanied by "volumes of historical text" that relate "a history of the official relations between the United States and these tribes."[2]

The maps of Cherokee land cessions developed by Royce are still used today. "The maps are intended to show not only the ancestral but the present home of the Cherokees, and also to indicate the boundaries of the various tracts of territory purchased from them by the Colonial or Federal authorities from time to time since their first contact with the European settlements." (Figure 1) Royce lists as his sources the "old manuscript records of the Government, the shelves of the Congressional Library, including its very large collection of American maps, local records, and the knowledge of 'old settlers,' as well as the accretions of various State historical societies..."[3]

Royce made his sympathies clear:

> For two hundred years a contest involving their very existence as a people had been maintained against the unscrupulous rapacity of Anglo-Saxon civilization. By degrees they were given from their ancestral domain to an unknown and inhospitable region. The country of their fathers was peculiarly dear to them.... The removal turned the Cherokees back in the calendar of progress and civilization at least a quarter of a century. The hardships and exposures of the journey, coupled with the fevers

1 Charles C. Royce, *The Cherokee Nation of Indians* (Chicago: Aldine Publishing Company, 1975).

2 Ibid., 1.

3 Ibid., 1-2.

> and malaria of a radically different climate, cost the lives of perhaps as much as 10 percent of their entire population...[4]

James Mooney, another ethnographer employed by the Smithsonian, lived between 1887 and 1890 among the Eastern Cherokee in North Carolina, recording their myths, sacred formulas, and history. Unlike Royce, his focus was not on treaties and land cessions, but on recording the "history, archeology, geographic nomenclature, personal names, botany, medicine, arts, home life, religion, songs, ceremonies, and language of the tribe." Mooney characterized the Cherokee as "probably the largest and most important tribe in the United States," and yet he says that "nothing has yet been written of their history or general ethnology…"[5] His work remains, over a century later, the quintessential source for Cherokee ethnographic material. His treatment of the Removal itself, while comprising only five pages, was at that time perhaps the most detailed account yet written.[6]

Mooney's focus was on the horror of the event. "The history of this Cherokee removal of 1838, as gleaned by the author from the lips of actors in the tragedy, may well exceed in weight of grief and pathos any other passage in American history." He, like Royce, strongly identified with the Cherokee and his account is romanticized, emotional, and highly sentimental. Since Mooney's account of the Removal process is still widely quoted today, it is worth including here in its entirety:[7]

> Under (General Winfield) Scott's orders the troops were disposed at various points throughout the Cherokee country, where stockade forts were erected for gathering in and holding the Indians preparatory to removal. From these, squads of troops were sent to search out with rifle and bayonet every small cabin hidden away in the coves or by the sides of mountain streams, to seize and bring in as prisoners all the occupants, however or wherever they might be found.

---

4 Ibid., 249-256.

5 James Mooney, *Myths of the Cherokees and Sacred Formulas of the Cherokees* (Nashville: Charles Elder, 1972), 11.

6 Ibid., 130-135.

7 Ibid., 130.

> Families at dinner were startled by the sudden gleam of bayonets in the doorway and rose up to be driven with blows and oaths along the weary miles of trail that led to the stockade. Men were seized in their fields or going along the road, women were taken from their wheels and children from their play. In many cases, in turning for one last look as they crossed the ridge, they saw their homes in flames, fired by the lawless rabble that followed on the heels of the soldiers to loot and pillage.[8]

Mooney also did much to popularize the story of Tsali or "Charley," a resistor who became mythologized in the annual dramatic production *Unto These Hills*, presented by the Eastern Band of Cherokee Indians. "All were not … submissive," Mooney said.[9] Tsali, on seeing his wife "prodded with bayonets," tried to wrest a weapon from a soldier and killed him in the process. The manhunt for Tsali and his family members was assisted by a group of Cherokees who, as related by Mooney, were allowed to remain behind following the Removal, forming the nucleus of what would become the Eastern Band of Cherokee Indians. (We now know that the origins of the Eastern Band of Cherokee Indians are a much longer and more complicated story.)

In the 1930s came the next wave of Cherokee historians, spurred in part by the centennial of the Removal. Grant Foreman published two seminal works, *Indian Removal: The Emigration of the Five Civilized Tribes of Indians*, and *The Five Civilized Tribes*. Published by the University of Oklahoma Press in 1932 and 1934, respectively, for many years these were considered the authoritative accounts of the Trail of Tears. Often described as dry or dispassionate, Foreman's factual account was thoroughly researched for the sources available to him during the time period. He covered the removals of the Choctaws, the Creeks, the Chickasaws, the Cherokees, and the Seminoles the so-called "Five Civilized Tribes." Sixty pages are devoted to the Cherokee, of which about one-third describes the Trail of Tears and the removal process. Although the Cherokee and many of the other tribes had "so far advanced in learning and culture as to establish themselves permanently

---

8 Ibid., 130.

9 Ibid., 131.

on the soil, build homes and farms, cultivate the land," etc., Foreman said he did not intend to "indict the people of the South for mistreatment of the Indians." Instead, Grant said, his aim was to relate "merely a candid account of the removal of these southern Indians, so that the reader may have a picture of that interesting and tragic enterprise as revealed by an uncolored day-by-day recital of events."[10]

Foreman was quickly followed by Angie Debo, who covered much of the same territory as Foreman but was much more impassioned. Even the title of her book, *And Still the Waters Run: The Betrayal of the Five Civilized Tribes*, served as a provocative indictment. Chapter titles like "The Grafter's Share" and "The White Man's Land System" also betrayed Debo's strong biases. She described the removal as an "orgy of exploitation" in her preface, that employed "criminal methods."[11] Much of her focus was not on the Indian removals themselves but on their after-effects, especially upon the Indians now living in the West.

At the same time that Foreman and Debo were publishing their works, a group of accomplished amateurs and local historians led by Robert Sparks Walker and John P. Brown, both of whom lived in East Tennessee (and who formed, along with Zella Armstrong and Penelope Johnson Allen, a strong Chattanooga-area contingent of Cherokee enthusiasts and document collectors), were also telling the Cherokee Removal story. These generally were not trained academic historians like Foreman and Debo nor were they ethnographers like Royce and Mooney, but their works were well-researched and covered aspects of Cherokee history and removal that had remained largely untouched until that point. Each researcher had an easy narrative style well suited to a general readership. Walker, a lawyer by training and journalist by profession, was interested primarily in the history of the Brainerd mission near Chattanooga,[12] while Brown had more expansive ambitions.

---

10 Grant Foreman, *Indian Removal: The Emigration of the Five Civilized Tribes of Indians* (Norman: University of Oklahoma Press, 1972), 13-14.

11 Angie Debo, *And Still the Waters Run: The Betrayal of the Five Civilized Tribes* (Princeton: Princeton University Press, 1972), x.

12 Robert Sparks Walker, *Torchlights to the Cherokees: The Brainerd Mission* (Johnson City: Overmountain Press, 1993).

His major work, *Old Frontiers*, was for many years the best source of information on the Chickamauga group of Cherokee who lived near Lookout Mountain. Brown's highly readable 570-page tome spans the entirety of recorded Cherokee history in the East, from the *entrada* of Hernando DeSoto in 1540 to the removal of 1838. Brown includes detailed maps of Cherokee towns, photographs of Cherokee sites, a dictionary of Cherokee words, a list of Cherokee land cessions, and copious quotes and excerpts from primary source material, including the Draper manuscripts and correspondence and diaries from the many missionaries who were stationed in the old Cherokee Nation. *Old Frontiers* "is not the story of the Indian removal, although that subject is treated incidentally," said Brown. "The book is an attempt to draw together from many sources an authentic story of the Cherokees, from earliest times. It is, mainly, the story of their struggle to hold the land of their fathers against white encroachment."[13]

Smithsonian-associated ethnographers continued making contributions during the 1930s, as well. Thomas M. N. Lewis and Madeline Kneberg wrote *Tribes That Slumber: Indians of the Tennessee Region*, which dealt largely with Cherokee prehistory. The book served as an overview of archaeological discoveries that had resulted from Tennessee Valley Authority hydroelectric dam building projects. Removal was mentioned only in passing.[14]

Two historians emerged midcentury with histories of the Cherokee people, Henry T. Malone with *Cherokees of the Old South* and Grace Steele Woodward with *The Cherokees*. Both studies were expansive in scope, covering the Cherokee history from DeSoto's first encounters up to removal (and, in the case of Woodward, up to the mid-20th century). Malone begins with the cringe-inducing chapter, "Primitive Forest Children," and presents what is essentially a "progressivist," nationalistic interpretation of Cherokee history, arguing that the "mixed-blood" elites helped to introduce what Malone calls the "white man's civilization" to the Cherokees

---

13 John P. Brown, *Old Frontiers* (Kingsport: Southern Publishers, 1938), vii.

14 Thomas M. N. Lewis and Madeline Kneberg, *Tribes that Slumber: Indians of the Tennessee Region* (Knoxville: University of Tennessee Press, 1986).

in the form of farming techniques, reading, writing, and industry. "At a moment of great promise for Indians moving impressively toward the white man's way of life, the white man obstructed that progress by thrusting the Cherokees out of their native lands."[15] While Malone totally ignores modern Cherokees, Woodward begins her book with a chapter titled "The Cherokees Today." However, she too adopts a progressivist and patronizing tone with her very first sentence: "The emergence of any primitive Indian tribe or nation from dark savagery into the sunlight of civilization is a significant event."[16] She devotes only one chapter, consisting of twenty-five pages, to the Trail of Tears itself. The primary Cherokee voices she reports are, on the one hand, wealthy elite leaders like Chief John Ross and high-ranking tribal officers, and "Treaty Party" leaders like John Ridge and Elias Boudinot on the other. Regarding the plight of everyday Cherokee farmers, she is mostly silent.

New social and feminist approaches to history were employed in the 1980s by historians like William G. McLoughlin and Theda Perdue. McLoughlin was largely concerned with Missionary-Cherokee interactions and the early "civilizing" policies of the George Washington administration and how those interactions influenced Cherokee nation-building, while Perdue focused on the role of women and clans in the traditional matrilineal society of the Cherokees. In his work, *Cherokees and Missionaries, 1789- 1839,* McLoughlin told the story of the "failure of the first Indian policy of the United States" through the eyes of the missionaries, employing a store of previously unmined primary source material.[17] McLoughlin expanded upon his work in *Cherokee Renascence in the New Republic,* exploring the same time frame from his previous book, but from a more Cherokee-centered political perspective.[18] He followed these works with a study of Cherokee political strife post-Removal,

15 Henry Thompson Malone, *Cherokees of the Old South* (Athens: University of Georgia Press, 1956), 184.

16 Grace Steele Woodward, *The Cherokees* (Norman: University of Oklahoma Press, 1963), 3.

17 William G. McLoughlin, *Cherokees and Missionaries, 1789-1839* (New Haven: Yale University Press, 1984).

18 William G. McLoughlin, *Cherokee Renascence in the New Republic* (Princeton: Princeton University Press, 1986).

After the Trail of Tears: The Cherokees' Struggle for Sovereignty, 1839-1880.[19] Neither McLoughlin nor Perdue focused much of their work on the Removal itself, although McLoughlin did write an article in which he tried to decipher the motivations Georgians had in removing the Cherokee people from their land, which included what he called a misreading of the Compact of 1802, coupled with the rise of romantic strains of nationalism.[20] Perdue authored an influential feminist study on the role of Cherokee women in Cherokee society in the years leading up to Removal,[21] while Perdue's primary book on the Removal itself, *The Cherokee Removal: A Brief History with Documents*, is essentially a heavily annotated compilation of primary source documents.[22] (She co-authored this work with Michael D. Green, along with an excellent brief overview of the Removal, *The Cherokee Nation and the Trail of Tears*, published in 2007.)[23] Vicki Rozema published a similar primary source compilation just prior to Perdue's, in 2003,[24] and Daniel F. Littlefield and James W. Parins followed with a multi-volume, expansive set of primary sources encompassing numerous tribes across the nation in 2011.[25] Littlefield and Parins said they were guided in their work by a challenge raised by Cherokee scholar Lathel Duffield in 2002, in his essay, "Cherokee Emigration: Reconstructing Reality." Duffield accused twentieth century Cherokee scholars and historians of spreading misinformation about the Cherokee Removal, and he urged them to go back to the primary sources and begin

---

19 William G. McLoughlin, *After the Trail of Tears: The Cherokees' Struggle for Sovereignty, 1839-1880* (Chapel Hill: The University of North Carolina Press, 1994).

20 William G. McLoughlin, "Georgia's Role in Instigating Compulsory Indian Removal." *Georgia Historical Quarterly* 70, no. 4 (1986): 605-632.

21 Theda Perdue, *Cherokee Women* (Lincoln: University of Nebraska Press, 1999).

22 Theda Perdue and Michael D. Green, *The Cherokee Removal: A Brief History with Documents* (Boston: Bedford / St. Martin's, 2005).

23 Theda Perdue and Michael D. Green, *The Cherokee Nation and the Trail of Tears* (New York: Penguin Books, 2008).

24 Vicki Rozema, *Voices from the Trail of Tears* (Winston-Salem: John F. Blair, 2003).

25 Daniel F. Littlefield and James W. Parins. *Encyclopedia of American Indian Removal* (Santa Barbara: Greenwood, 2011).

again.[26] (In fact by far the most popular and widely available account of the Trail of Tears published during the past several decades has been John Ehle's *Trail of Tears: The Rise and Fall of the Cherokee Nation,* which is as much speculative fiction as it is a history book).[27] While these volumes published over the past decade-and-a-half are exceedingly helpful and important steps toward addressing Duffield's concerns, for whatever reason all of these historians have neglected to include the Cherokee claims from 1842 that describe the Removal event from the Cherokee layman's perspective.

One of the better treatments of the Cherokee Removal is another edited volume, by William L. Anderson, published in 1991, titled *Cherokee Removal: Before and After*. Douglas C. Wilms contributes an essay on Cherokee land use, while other contributors focus on the rhetoric of Andrew Jackson, the impact of Removal on North Carolina Cherokees, and the post-Removal lives of Cherokees. Perdue discusses the conflict between treaty advocates and traditionalists.[28] But perhaps the most interesting contribution is made by demographer Russell Thornton, "The Demography of the Trail of Tears: A New Estimate of Cherokee Population Losses," which he later expanded into a full-length book, *The Cherokees: A Population History*. He estimated that as many as 100,000 Native Americans were removed from their homelands in the Southeast, and that the "demographic devastation of Cherokee removal was far more severe than has yet been realized." Thornton concluded that over 10,000 additional Cherokees would have been alive during the Removal period had the Removal not occurred.[29]

Duane King also authored an overview of the Removal, *The Cherokee Trail of Tears,* as part of text development for an exhibition of photographs by David G. Fitzgerald. The extended essay, published double-spaced in book form,

---

26 Duffield, Lathel F. "Cherokee Emigration: Reconstructing Reality." *The Chronicles of Oklahoma 80* (Fall 2002): 314–347.
27 John Ehle, *Trail of Tears: The Rise and Fall of the Cherokee Nation* (New York: Anchor Books, 1988).
28 William L. Anderson, ed., *Cherokee Removal: Before and After* (Athens: University of Georgia Press, 1991).
29 Russell Thornton, *The Cherokees: A Population History* (Lincoln: University of Nebraska Press, 1990).

provides a general narrative overview of the Treaty of New Echota, the various routes and detachments, along with some statistics. King traces general routes taken by various detachments and puts those into the form of a linear narrative. As in other accounts of the Removal, the primary sources used are, for the most part, from the official papers of Chief John Ross, contemporary newspaper accounts, and most especially from the white missionaries like Daniel Butrick who traveled with the Cherokees on their journey west.[30]

Gender continued to provide a useful lens for scholars studying the Cherokee in the 1990s, most notably in Sarah H. Hill's *Weaving New Worlds*, an examination of Cherokee women and their basketry. Hill looked at Cherokee life through the roles of women in Cherokee society, and especially through their basket weaving. She contextualized this through extensive interviews with contemporary Cherokees and also through the interspersing of the Cherokee myths collected by Mooney as a framing and contextual device.[31] Removal was hardly mentioned. However, in a report written by Hill for the National Park Service and the Georgia Department of Natural Resources in 2005, Cherokee Removal from Georgia was Hill's primary focus, and she extensively mined the archival record, probably more than anyone ever had before, drafting what amounted to a brief military history.[32] Hill has also authored articles [33] and delivered papers at conferences on removal forts and military operations at Fort Hetzel in Ellijay,[34] Sixes at Lake Allatoona,[35] Cedar Town encampment,[36] Camp Malone at

30 Duane King, *The Cherokee Trail of Tears* (Portland: Graphic Arts Books, 2007).

31 Sarah H. Hill, *Weaving New Worlds: Southeastern Cherokee Women and their Basketry* (Chapel Hill: University of North Carolina Press, 1997).

32 http://www.nps.gov/trte/historyculture/upload/Georgia-Forts.pdf

33 Sarah H. Hill, "To Overawe the Indians and Give Confidence to the Whites: Preparations for the Removal of the Cherokee Nation from Georgia." *Georgia Historical Quarterly* 95, no. 4 (2011):465-497.

34 http://www.southernspaces.org/2012/cherokee-removal-scenes-ellijay-georgia-1838

35 http://vimeo.com/46884161

36 http://trailofthetrail.blogspot.com/2009/11/newly-revised-site-report-for-cedartown.html

Rome,[37] and other Removal-related sites. Archaeologist Ronald Hobgood investigated a number of those sites as part of his master's thesis and for a follow-up report for the National Park Service.[38]

Scholars of the Jacksonian Era – most notably Robert V. Remini — have also tackled the issue of Indian Removal, a major campaign issue and policy initiative of Andrew Jackson. Remini, in *Andrew Jackson and His Indian Wars,* tried to couch the Indian Removal issue within the cultural and political context of its time. Remini controversially argued that Removal may have been the best option for the Cherokees, and may have actually saved them from being exterminated.[39] While some see merit in Remini's arguments, the continued existence of the Eastern Band of Cherokee Indians in North Carolina, who managed to evade Removal, offers a powerful counterpoint. Still, Remini's study represents a step forward in the discourse. (For many decades the most popular work on Jackson was the Pulitzer Prize-winning *Age of Jackson* by Arthur Schlesinger, Jr. —a work that barely makes any mention of Indians at all.)[40]

New interpretations of Cherokee history have been put forward by Tiya Miles and Tyler Boulware. Miles uses race, gender, and class to frame her works, which earned her a MacArthur Foundation grant. She is especially interested in one facet of Cherokee assimilation of European cultural forms—slave ownership and plantation establishment by wealthy Cherokees—and how that affected notions of identity formation and agency among various groups of people living in the Cherokee Nation in the early nineteenth century. Miles uses a rich variety of source material, but limits her scope to narrow areas of study, such as a single family living on the Etowah River, in the case of *Ties that Bind,*[41] or a plantation

---

37 https://southernspaces.org/2017/all-roads-led-rome-facing-history-cherokee-expulsion

38 Ronald Hobgood, "The First Tears of the Trail: Archaeological Investigations of Potential Cherokee Removal Fort Sites in Georgia." *Early Georgia* 37, No. 1 (2009): 101-131.

39 Robert V. Remini, *Andrew Jackson and his Indian Wars* (New York: Penguin Books, 2002).

40 Arthur M. Schlesinger, Jr, *The Age of Jackson* (New York: Little, Brown, 1945).

41 Tiya Miles, *Ties that Bind: The Story of an Afro-American*

owned by a wealthy Cherokee, in *The House on Diamond Hill*.[42] While Miles followed Perdue and Hill in emphasizing the importance gender and class played in the Cherokee experiences of the period, Boulware went an entirely different direction and argued that the importance of the Cherokee concept of "town" has been largely neglected. He rightfully points out that in the primary source documents of the eighteenth century notable figures like Attakullakulla and Old Hop are inextricably associated with their towns, and that they publicly link themselves with their towns in their speeches and messages. The town was the level at which important decisions were made, at which ceremonies were observed, and at which petitions were joined, he says. In response to violent interactions with the Creeks, the Iroquois, and the English, sometimes town sites or even entire regions had to be abandoned for a time, in which case the old name may have been retained, or an entirely new town may have been formed. This constant shifting and overall tenuousness of the traditional town unit may have led to an increased awareness and heightened importance of a kind of "national" Cherokee identity, especially after the migrations of Dragging Canoe and his followers to the new "Five Lower Towns" near Lookout Mountain. As the old lands and old mounds and town houses were increasingly abandoned, new ideas of identity began to be explored, including ideas of national identity, modeled on those of the Europeans.[43] Although both Miles and Boulware have contributed important new ideas to the discourse, neither scholar particularly emphasizes Indian Removal in their works.

Hill is working on a new book specifically about the Cherokee Removal, but her work (as I understand it) will narrowly focus on Georgia, and especially on Fort Wool at New Echota and its military operations. "Rather than a military history (where I started) the book has become

---

Family in Slavery and Freedom (Berkeley: University of California Press, 2006).

42 Tiya Miles, *The House on Diamond Hill: A Cherokee Plantation Story* (Chapel Hill: The University of North Carolina Press, 2012).

43 Tyler Boulware, *Deconstructing the Cherokee Nation: Town, Region, and Nation among Eighteenth Century Cherokees* (Gainesville: University Press of Florida, 2011).

an examination of how and why Georgia led the nation in the initiative to expel the Cherokees," Hill said. "The 'why' is deep history but the 'how' identifies Georgia participants and their motives … the book, Called *Taking Place: the Removal of the Cherokee Nation from Georgia,* has New Echota as the flashpoint."[44] Hill has described her latest work as "set(ting) the record straight" following years of "inadequate documentation of the removal process," which has led to "simplified and sentimental accounts of villainous soldiers, helpless or hostile Cherokees, and greedy Georgia bystanders." As she states in a recent online article:

> Recent research into the details of Cherokee removal from Georgia reveals a more complex process, identifies participants at each post, documents their roles and activities, and establishes a calendar of events. Such new information neither absolves the federal government of its treachery in obtaining a removal treaty, dismisses the criminal aggression of individual Georgians, nor disregards the extraordinary loss the Cherokees experienced. Rather, the records provide substance and texture to a singular moment in history that serves as historical corrective and cautionary tale...
>
> Emerging details reveal its complexities and call for a deeper engagement of a singular historical tragedy… They bring to light the missing names and locations, activities and events, attitudes and motivations that make the history of Cherokee removal from Georgia a living and relevant discourse for the present. [45]

One of these "simplified and sentimental accounts" is the widely published John G. Burnett "birthday story." On December 11, 1890, on his 80th birthday, a white man named Burnett (or more likely his children) wrote down for posterity an emotional tale of Cherokee women "dragged from their homes by soldiers whose language they could not understand," and of "sad-faced" children dying in the arms of their parents, to be buried in shallow graves by the roadside. The account is vivid in its details – Burnett claims to

---

44 Sarah Hill, personal communication.

45 https://southernspaces.org/2012/cherokee-removal-scenes-ellijay-georgia-1838

be an eyewitness, serving in the mounted infantry during the Removal. Burnett tells of Ross' wife, Quatie Ross, dying from exposure after giving her only blanket to a sick child while riding through a snow storm. He adopts a self-righteous tone as he condemns the United States of committing murder. "… (M)urder is murder whether committed by the villain skulking in the dark or by uniformed men stepping to the strains of martial music," Burnett wrote. Somebody "must answer, somebody must explain the streams of blood that flowed in the Indian country in the summer of 1838." Burnett excuses himself from his charges, saying, "I did my best for them when they certainly did need a friend, "even going so far as to learn the Cherokee language and serving as an interpreter." [46] From an emotional standpoint, and as a cultural "meme," the Burnett birthday story has to be recognized as a tremendous success. I found it included in my fourth-grader's social studies book, and it has been used in course materials at the University of West Georgia as recently as last year. Searching for Burnett's story on the Google search engine will yield over 10 million results. Johnny Cash crafted it into a recording.[47] It's even featured on the Cherokee Nation's official web site.[48]

But the Burnett story is a complete fabrication. Quatie Ross could not have died as Burnett describes it, because she removed to the West by water and is buried at a well-marked grave in Little Rock, Arkansas. Burnett could not have accompanied the Cherokees to the West during the winter because by that time the Cherokees themselves were overseeing their own Removal, under the direction of John Ross, and soldiers were in no way involved. Burnett's own military records indicate he mustered out of service prior to the Removal. While we cannot know his motivations, Burnett's birthday story is certainly a fiction.[49]

---

46 John G. Burnett, "The Cherokee Removal Through the Eyes of a Private Soldier." *Journal of Cherokee Studies* 3, no. 3 (1978): 50-55.

47 https://www.youtube.com/watch?v=qW8rIM2lNN8

48 www.cherokee.org/AboutTheNation/History/TrailofTears/JohnBurnettsStoryoftheTrailofTears.aspx

49 For more information on the "Private John G. Burnett Fable," see the research of Jerry Clark and also Kirk Johnson, *Cherokee Removal Primer* (self published, 2016), 72-89.

As if suffering the forced appropriation of their lands were not enough, the Cherokee also must suffer this final act of appropriation – the theft of their own story, the displacement of their voice.

Oo-loo-cha, the widow of Sweet Water, is one such voice. If one were to search for her on the Internet, she barely registers. Her tale (first captured in the untranscribed compilations of Marybelle Chase and utilized to great effect by Hill in her report on Georgia forts) is not as romanticized and bombastic as Burnett's, but it has the advantage of being immediate and true:

> The soldiers came and took us from home. They first surrounded our house and they took the mare while we were at work in the fields and they drove us out of doors and did not permit us to take anything with us, not even a second change of clothes... They marched us to Ross' Landing, and still on foot, even our little children, and they sent us off."[50]

There are many more such stories, thousands of them in fact, told by ordinary Cherokees who reported their trials in the *Cherokee Phoenix* newspaper, or recorded them in letters and journals or school assignments, or filed their claims for damages against the United States government. Many of these stories have not been transcribed before and generally are not told. This book aims to restore Cherokee voice to the Removal by utilizing some of these untapped primary sources, as urged by Duffield nearly two decades ago, serving as another step forward in constructing a completely new social history of the event known as the Trail of Tears.

---

50 Marybelle W. Chase, *1842 Cherokee Claims: Skin Bayou District* (from original claims located at the Tennessee State Library and Archives, Nashville, Tennessee), 210-211.

'Their whole cry is more land'

Dragging Canoe

Chief of Amoyeliegwa (Great Island)

March, 1775

From a speech given at Sycamore Shoals

Whole Indian Nations have melted away like snowballs in the sun before the white man's advance…

We had hoped the white men would not be willing to travel beyond the mountains. Now that hope is gone. They have passed the mountains, and have settled upon Cherokee land. They wish to have that usurpation sanctioned by treaty. When that is gained, the same encroaching spirit will lead them upon other land of the Cherokees. New sessions will be asked. Finally the whole country, which the Cherokees and their fathers have so long occupied, will be demanded, and the remnant of the Ani-Yunwiya, 'The Real People,' once so great and formidable, will be compelled to seek refuge in some distant wilderness. There they will be permitted to stay only a short while, until they again behold the advancing banners of the same greedy host. Not being able to point out any further retreat for the miserable Cherokees, the extinction of the whole race will be proclaimed. Should we not therefore run all risks, and incur all consequences, rather than submit to further laceration of our country? Such treaties may be all right for men who are too old to hunt or fight. As for me, I have my young warriors about me. We will have our lands. *A-waninski*, I have spoken.[51]

51 John P. Brown, *Old Frontiers* (Kingsport: Southern Publishers, 1938), 9-10. http://www.learnnc.org/lp/editions/nchist-revolution/4301

Old Tassel

Long Island on the Holston River

July, 1777

It is surprising that when we enter into treaties with our fathers the white people, their whole cry is more land. Indeed it has seemed a formality with them to demand what they know we dare not refuse. But on the principles of fairness of which we have received assurance during the conduct of this treaty, I must refuse your demand.

What did you do? You marched into our towns with a superior force. Your numbers far exceeded us, and we fled to the stronghold of our woods, there to secure our women and children. Our towns were left to your mercy. You killed a few scattered and defenseless individuals, spread fire and desolation wherever you pleased, and returned to your own habitations...

Much has been said of the want of what you term 'Civilization' among the Indians. Many proposals have been made to us to adopt your laws, your religion, your manners, and your customs. We do not see the propriety of such a reformation. We should be better pleased with beholding the good effect of these doctrines in your own practices than with hearing you talk about them...

The Great Spirit has placed us in different situations. He has given you many advantages, but he has not created us to be your slaves.[52]

---

52 Ibid., 166-167. http://www.historyisaweapon.com/defcon1/corntassel.html

The Treaty of Hopewell

November 28, 1785

The boundary allotted to the Cherokees for their hunting grounds, between the said Indians and the citizens of the United States, within the limits of the United States of America, is, and shall be the following, viz. Beginning at the mouth of Duck river, on the Tennessee; thence running north-east to the ridge dividing the waters running into Cumberland from those running into the Tennessee; thence east-wardly along the said ridge to a north-east line to be run, which shall strike the river Cumberland forty miles above Nashville; thence along the said line to the river; thence up the said river to the ford where the Kentucky road crosses the river; thence to Campbell's line, near Cumberland gap; thence to the mouth of Claud's creek on Holstein; thence to the Chimney-top mountain; thence to Camp-creek, near the mouth of Big Limestone, on Nolichuckey; thence a southerly course six miles to a mountain; thence south to the North-Carolina line; thence to the South-Carolina Indian boundary, and along the same south-west over the top of the Oconee mountain till it shall strike Tugaloo river; thence a direct line to the top of the Currohee mountain; thence to the head of the south fork of Oconee river.[53]

53 Shawnee Nation, Cherokee Nation. 1785 Nov. 28, and Continental Congress Broadside Collection. Articles of a treaty, concluded at the mouth of the Great Miami, on the north-western bank of the Ohio, the thirty-first of January, one thousand seven hundred and eighty-six, between the commissioners plenipotentiary of the United States of America, of the one part, and the chiefs and warriors of the Shawanoe Nation of the other part. [New York: s.n, 1786] https://www.loc.gov/item/90898246/

Henry Knox

US. Secretary of War

June 15, 1798

The Indians being the prior occupants, possess the right of the soil. It cannot be taken from them unless by their free consent, or by the right of conquest in case of a just war. To dispossess them on any other principle, would be a gross violation of the fundamental laws of nature, and of that distributive justice which is the glory of a nation.[54]

54 American State Papers: Indian Affairs, I: 13 https://memory.loc.gov/cgi-bin/ampage?collId=llsp&fileName=007/llsp007.db&recNum=14

Henry Knox

U.S. Secretary of War

A letter to President George Washington

July 7, 1789

Although the disposition of the people of the States to emigrate into the Indian country cannot be effectually prevented, it may be restrained and regulated.

The disgraceful violation of the Treaty of Hopewell with the Cherokees requires the serious consideration of Congress – If so direct and manifest contempt of the authority of the United States be suffered with impunity, it will be in vain to attempt to extend the arm of Government to the frontiers – The Indian tribes can have no faith in such imbecile promises, and the lawless whites will ridicule a Government which shall on paper only, make Indian treaties and regulate the indian boundaries.

It is however painful to consider that all the Indian Tribes once existing in those States, now the best cultivated and most populous, have become extinct. If the same causes continue, the same effects will happen, and in a Short period the Idea of an Indian on this side of the Mississippi will only be found in the page of the historian...

How different would be the sensation of a philosophic mind to reflect that instead of exterminating a part of the human race by our modes of population that we had persevered through all difficulties and at last had imparted our Knowledge of cultivation, and the arts, to the Aboriginals of the Country by which the Source of future life and happiness had been preserved and extended. But it has been conceived to be impracticable to civilize the Indians of North America – This opinion is probably more convenient than Just.

That the civilization of the indians would be an operation of complicated difficulty. That it would require the highest knowledge of the human character, and a Steady persiverance in a wise system for a series of years cannot be doubted – But to deny that under a course of favorable circumstances it could not be accomplished is to suppose the human character under the influence of such stubborn habits as to be incapable of melioration or change – a supposition entirely contradicted by the progress of society from the barbarous ages to its present degree of perfection.

Were it possible to introduce among the Indian tribes a love for exclusive property it would be a happy commencement of the business.

Missionaries of excellent moral character should be appointed to reside in their nation, who should be well supplied with all the implements of husbandry and the necessary stock for a farm.

Such a plan although it might not fully effect the civilization of the Indians would most probably be attended with the salutary effect of attaching them to the Interest of the United States.

It is particularly important that something of this nature should be attempted with the southern nations of indians, whose confined situation might render them proper subjects for the experiment.[55]

55 American State Papers: Indian Affairs, I, No. 4: 53 https://memory.loc.gov/cgi-bin/ampage?collId=llsp&fileName=007/llsp007.db&recNum=54

George Washington

US. President

1796

I believe scarcely anything short of a Chinese Wall, or a line of Troops, will restrain Land jobbers, and the encroachment of Settlers upon the Indian Territory.[56]

56 "George Washington to the Secretary of State, 1 July 1796," *The Writings of George Washington*, 35:112. http://www.mountvernon.org/digital-encyclopedia/article/native-american-policy/

The Compact of 1802

...the United States shall, at their own expense, extinguish, for the use of Georgia, as early as the same can be peaceably obtained, on reasonable terms, ... the Indian title to all the ... lands within the State of Georgia.[57]

57 American State Papers: Public Lands, I: 114 https://memory.loc.gov/cgi-bin/ampage?collId=llsp&fileName=028/llsp028.db&recNum=123 Additional information: http://trailofthetrail.blogspot.com/2011/02/compact-of-1802-too-often-ignored.html

Thomas Jefferson

US. President

January 10, 1806

The Mississippi now belongs to us.... That country is ours. We will permit them to live on it.[58]

58 The writings of Thomas Jefferson, Volumes 19-20 By Thomas Jefferson, Richard Holland Johnston, Thomas Jefferson Memorial Association of the United States, 148-149 http://millercenter.org/president/jefferson/speeches/speech-3494

Thomas Jefferson

US. President

January 9, 1809

I understand by speeches you have delivered me that there is a difference of disposition among people in both parts of your nation. Some of them desiring to remain on their land, to betake themselves to agriculture and the industrious occupations of civilized life, while others retaining their attachment to the hunter's life, and having little game on their present lands, are desirous to remove across the Mississippi to some of the vacant land of the U.S. (United States) where game is abundant. I am pleased to find so many disposed to insure, by cultivation of the earth a plentiful subsistence to their families, and to improve their minds by education, but I do not blame those who having been brought from their infancy to the pursuit of game, desire still to follow it to distant countries. I know how difficult it is to change the habits to which they have been raised. The U.S. (United States), My Children, are the friends of both parties and as far as can reasonably be asked, they will be willing to satisfy the wishes of both. Those who remain may be of our patronage, our aid and good neighborhood — those who wish to remove are permitted to send an exploring party to reconnoitre the country…[59]

---

59 American State Papers: Indian Affairs II: 125 https://memory.loc.gov/cgi-bin/ampage?collId=llsp&fileName=008/llsp008.db&recNum=132

James Monroe

U.S. President

From a conversation with Cherokees

As reported by Sam Houston

1817

You are now in a country where you can be happy; no white man shall ever again disturb you...the white shall never again encroach upon you, and you will have a great outlet to the West.

As long as water flows, or grass grows upon the earth, or the sun rises to show your pathway, or you kindle your camp fires, so long shall you be protected from your present habitations.[60]

---

60 Stan Hoig, *Beyond the Frontier: Exploring the Indian Country* (Norman: University of Oklahoma Press, 1998), 11. Speech by Senator Sam Houston, U.S. Congressional Globe, Appendix, 33rd Congress, 1st session, Feb. 14-15, 1854. https://www.edmondhistory.org/as-long-as-grass-grows/

Cherokee National Council

Pronouncement

1823

It is the fixed and unalterable determination of this nation never again to cede one foot more of our land.[61]

61 Ulrich Bonnell Phillips, *Georgia and State Rights: A Study of the Political History of Georgia from the Revolution to the Civil War*, Vol. II (Washington: Government Printing Office, 1902), 69. http://www.randomhouse.com/highschool/catalog/display.pperl?isbn=9780307390837&view=excerpt

Nancy and Alecy, daughters of Dick-es-sky

Su-wo-ne Town, Chattahoochee River

1820

Our father in his lifetime (lived in 1820) in Su Wo Ne Town Old Nation...on the Chattahoochee River. And the hewn log house and three hundred bushels of wheat … was burnt and destroyed by some white men who set the house on fire. The fifteen acres of growing corn was cut down by the Intruders in 1820. After the Troops had cut down the intruders' corn … our father was drove and forced by the white people same year to move off and leave all that he had behind, which our father done, and he never got anything for his property which he left at that place.[62]

62 Marybelle W. Chase, *1842 Cherokee Claims, Goingsnake District* (from originals located at the Tennessee State Library and Archives, Nashville, Tennessee), 37-38.

Thomas Petit

Cherokee Nation citizen

Two Runs Village

(near present-day Kingston, GA)

Testimony taken on December 14, 1829

I, Thomas Petit, mixed blood Cherokee and white, think I am about 61 years of age, was born and raised on the head waters of Chattahoochy until I was thirteen or fourteen years old, towards the close of the Revolutionary War. General Pickens with an army burnt the town of Chota and Sorta two villages on the Chattahoochy- I was taken prisoner with my mother and many others, but the General left my mother and myself in the nation when he took most of the prisoners away with him. Shortly after that my mother left that part of the country and moved down the Hightower River and settled the place called the Red Bank. We were among the first settlers of that town. After living there some years when I was nearly grown, my mother moved about twenty miles to the Pine Log Village, where I have lived and in the neighborhood of the same place ever since. A great many years ago there was a treaty held at Fort Wilkinson between the whites and Creeks, and the head chiefs of our nation were afraid the Creeks would sell some of our lands and sent old Sour Mush, old Chulio, Old Turkey and Eutalitta to attend the treaty and try to make a line with the Creeks; and they sent old Segawee with them to interpret between the Cherokees and Creeks, and they sent Dick Rowe to interpret between the Cherokees and the whites. General Pickens and Col. Hawkins were Commissioners who held the treaty. After they came back from the treaty, old Sour Mush told me that they had agreed upon a line with the Creeks, that at first they differed a little; the Cherokees proposed to make the old Cherokee Corner the beginning corner of their country, but the Creeks refused to go so far back, but proposed to let the Cherokees begin at the High shoals of Appalachy which the Cherokees agreed to. They agreed the line should run from there to the Ten Islands on the Coosa River, so as to leave the Stone Mountain on the Cherokee lands. I have always understood among the Cherokees that they owned the country on both sides of the Coosa River as low as the Ten Islands. I was one of the commissioners for the Cherokee Nation who marked the line between the two nations in 1822, which had been agreed on in 1821. This is the only line I ever heard of between the two nations which said line runs from Buzzard Roost on the Chattahoochy to the mouth of Will›s Creek on the Coosa River.[63]

63 *Cherokee Phoenix,* May 22, 1830. http://www.wcu.edu/library/DigitalCollections/CherokeePhoenix/Vol3/no05/3n05-p1-c1b.htm

Elias Boudinot

From "An Address to the Whites"

Delivered at the First Presbyterian Church

May 26, 1826

It is a matter of surprise to me, and must be to all those who are properly acquainted with the condition of the Aborigines of this country, that the Cherokees have advanced so far and so rapidly in civilization. But there are yet powerful obstacles, both within and without, to be surmounted in the march of improvement. The prejudices in regard to them in the general community are strong and lasting. The evil effects of their intercourse with their immediate white neighbours, who differ from them chiefly in name, are easily to be seen, and it is evident that from this intercourse proceed those demoralizing practices which in order to surmount, peculiar and unremitting efforts are necessary. In defiance, however, of these obstacles the Cherokees have improved and are still rapidly improving. To give you a further view of their condition, I will here repeat some of the articles of the two statistical tables taken at different periods.

In 1810 There were 19,500 cattle; 6,100 horses; 19,600 swine; 1,037 sheep; 467 looms; 1,600 spinning wheels; 30 waggons; 500 ploughs; 3 saw-mills; 13 grist-mills &c. At this time there are 22,000 cattle; 7,600 Horses; 46,000 swine; 2,500 sheep; 762 looms; 2488 spinning wheels; 172 waggons; 2,943 ploughs; 10 saw-mills; 31 grist-mills; 62 Blacksmith-shops; 8 cotton machines; 18 schools; 18 ferries; and a number of public roads. In one district there were, last winter, upwards of 0000 volumes of good books; and 11 different periodical papers both religious and political, which were taken and read. On the public roads there are many decent Inns, and few houses for convenience, &c., would disgrace any country. Most of the schools are under the care and tuition of christian missionaries, of different denominations, who have been of great service to the nation, by inculcating moral and religious principles into the minds of the rising generation. In many places the word of God is regularly preached and explained, both by missionaries and natives; and there are numbers who have publicly professed their belief and interest in the merits of the great Saviour of the world. It is worthy of remark, that in no ignorant country have the missionaries undergone less trouble and difficulty, in spreading a knowledge of the Bible, than in this. Here, they have been welcomed and encouraged by the proper authorities of the nation, their persons have been protected, and in very few instances have some individual vagabonds threatened violence to them. Indeed it may be said with truth, that among no heathen people has the faithful minister of God experienced greater success, greater reward for his labour, than in this.[64]

64 Theda Perdue, ed., *Cherokee Editor: The Writings of Elias Boudinot* (Athens: University of Georgia Press, 1983), 72-73. https://archive.org/details/addresstooOboud

John Ridge

Secretary to the Cherokee Nation

You asked us to throw off the hunter and warrior state: We did so – you asked us to form a republican government: We did so – adopting your own as a model. You asked us to cultivate the earth, and learn the mechanic arts: We did so. You asked us to learn to read: We did so. You asked us to cast away our idols, and worship your God: We did so.[65]

65 John Ehle, *Trail of Tears: The Rise and Fall of the Cherokee Nation* (New York: Anchor Books, 1988), 254. http://articles.latimes.com/1988-09-11/books/bk-2871_1_cherokee-nation

George M. Troup

Governor of Georgia

From a letter to John Forsyth,

US. Congressman from Georgia

April 6, 1825

The Cherokees must be told, in plain language, that the lands they occupy belong to Georgia ... Why conceal from them the fact that every advance in the improvement of the country is to ensure to the benefit of Georgia; that every fixture will pass with the soil into our hands, sooner or later .... The United States are bound, in justice to themselves, instantly to arrest the progress of improvement in the Cherokee country; it is the reason constantly assigned by the Cherokees for their refusal to abandon the country.[66]

66 American State Papers: Indian Affairs II: 776 http://quod.lib.umich.edu/cgi/t/text/text-idx?c=moa&cc=moa&view=text&rgn=main&idno=ABT3932.0001.001

James Monroe

U.S. President

1825 Message to Congress

Being deeply impressed with the opinion that the removal of the Indian tribes from the lands which they now occupy within the limits of the several states and Territories . . . is of very high importance to our Union, and may be accomplished on conditions and in a manner to promote the interest and happiness of those tribes, the attention of the Government has been long drawn with great solicitude to the object. For the removal of the tribes within the limits of the State of Georgia the motive has been peculiarly strong, arising from the compact with that State whereby the United States are bound to extinguish the Indian title to the lands within it whenever it may be done peaceably and on reasonable conditions. . . .

The removal of the tribes from the territory which they now inhabit . . . would not only shield them from impending ruin, but promote their welfare and happiness. Experience has clearly demonstrated that in their present state it is impossible to incorporate them in such masses, in any form whatever, into our system. It has also demonstrated with equal certainty that without a timely anticipation of and provision against the dangers to which they are exposed, under causes which it will be difficult, if not impossible to control, their degradation and extermination will be inevitable.[67]

---

67 Steven Mintz, ed., *Native American Voices: A History and Anthology* (New York: Brandywine Press, 1995), 111-112. http://www.columbia.edu/~lmg21/BC3180/removal.html

A Young Cherokee

The closing part of an address

New Orleans

Summer of 1826

But gentlemen tell us that these Indians must be removed to some point in the west. What? Shall we leave our country, the gift of Heaven and the bequest of our ancestors? Forever bid farewell to the land that gave us birth — the pure and sweet waters of Tsalagi, and go to penetrate the dreary and inhospitable regions of the west? there to linger out a miserable existence? Never! never! Let us remain in the land of our Fathers, & give us death. We have resolved never to raise up arms against the United States, and if, in the course of time, that power were to aim at the extirpation of our race in order to get our lands, we shall willingly fall by our fire sides, and mingle our dust with that of our departed friends. We will seal the honor of our name at the altar of patriotism. Our spirits will go to the land of shadows, where our Fathers have gone, and where we hope to be annoyed no more by the avarice of the white man, who knows no law but that of power.

But I have forgotten myself. The Inspiration of my theme has carried me too far. I am addressing myself to a patriotic, enlightened, and christian assembly. I have anticipated events, which I hope, may never occur. For my brethren and kindred, the Cherokees are in the midst of a christian community, and in the bosom of the United States. Behold, I am at this moment, not in the dominions of the Sultan, & in a mahometan mosque, but in a land of freedom, pure christianity and enlightened benevolence, with the walls of a temple dedicated to an Almighty & a righteous God.

...Your friendly hand is extended to foreigners from every part of the Globe. Here the oppressed and persecuted in other nations find an asylum and a home. They are admitted, in time, into the rights and privileges of American citizens. In a word, your country is celebrated for the mildness of its government, the hospitality and humanity of its citizens, and for its superior religion, based on these words: «Do unto others as ye would they should do unto you.»

Surely then, you cannot concur in the policy of the day to remove the natives, the rightful and original owners of America, tantalized with hopes of civilization, from the native homes, to the wilds of the west. You will not, I am sure, aid in the destruction of the Cherokees and extinguish the last ray of hope left to them — strip them of every right, and all that is dear and precious to their hearts. — But such a project is in operation.... I invoke the genius of the Constitution of the United States, for protection.[68]

68 *Cherokee Phoenix*, March 11, 1829. http://www.wcu.edu/library/DigitalCollections/CherokeePhoenix/Vol1/no52/pg2col5b.htm

'Build fires around them...'

Andrew Jackson

US. President

First annual message to Congress

December 8, 1829

Our conduct toward these people is deeply interesting to our national character. Their present condition, contrasted with what they once were, makes a most powerful appeal to our sympathies. Our ancestors found them the uncontrolled possessors of these vast regions. By persuasion and force they have been made to retire from river to river and from mountain to mountain, until some of the tribes have become extinct and others have left but remnants to preserve for a while their once terrible names. Surrounded by the whites with their arts of civilization, which by destroying the resources of the savage doom him to weakness and decay, the fate of the Mohigan, the Narragansett and the Delaware is fast overtaking the Choctaw, the Cherokee, and the Creek. That this fate surely awaits them if they remain within the limits of the States does not admit of a doubt.

... I suggest for your consideration the propriety of setting apart an ample district west of the Mississippi, and without the limits of any State or Territory now formed, to be guaranteed to the Indian tribes as long as they shall occupy it, ...There the benevolent may endeavor to teach them the arts of civilization, and, by promoting union and harmony among them, to raise up an interesting commonwealth, destined to perpetuate the race and to attest the humanity and justice of this Government.

The emigration should be voluntary, for it would be as cruel as unjust to compel the aborigines to abandon the graves of their fathers and seek a home in a distant land. But they should be distinctly informed that if they remain within the limits of the States they must be subject to their laws. In return for their obedience as individuals they will without doubt be protected in the enjoyment of those possessions which they have improved by their industry. But it seems to me visionary to suppose that in this state of things claims can be allowed on tracts of country on which they have neither dwelt nor made improvements, merely because they have seen them from the mountain or passed them in the chase.[69]

---

69 Edward Walker, *The Addresses and Messages of the Presidents of the United States, from Washington to Harrison* (Boston: Little and Brown, 1841), 368-369. http://www.learnnc.org/lp/editions/nchist-newnation/4350

Outalissi

Cherokee Phoenix

January 6, 1830

From the Savannah Georgian

The Head Chiefs of the twenty-four Council-fires, President Jackson, has delivered his annual talk. In it he paints in true colors our treatment by the white-men—but all his talk results in this, that we must either abandon our country, or be subject to the tyranny of the State of Georgia—slavery or exile is the only alternative which he presents. Listen to his words ... This is so much like the expression of humane sentiments and generous feelings, that we are naturally prepared to expect, that at every hazard the faith of treaties in our favor will be upheld, that our rights will be protected and our beloved country, never ceded, never conquered, in our possession time immemorial, that it will be secured to us. But mark the end—"It is too late to inquire," continues the talk, "whether it was just in the United States to include them and their territory within the bounds of new States whose limits they could control. That step cannot be retraced—a State cannot be dismembered by Congress or restricted in the exercise of its Constitutional power."

Therefore as a State cannot be dismembered, she has a right to take our lands and tyranize over us that never justly formed any part of her members. On! generous conclusion, — reasoning as humane as it is accurate, — logic worthy of the white man! What is the meaning of the following words, the 7th article of our treaty in 1791 with Washington, still in force. "The United States solemnly guarantee TO THE CHEROKEE NATION all their lands not hereby ceded."

Has it come to this, that a President of the United States shall declare that it is too late to abide by the pledge solemnly given by Washington, for the integrity of our country? Do we live to see the day that his plighted faith, plighted, in the most binding and imposing form—pledged too in conjunction with that of those men who gave existence to this great Republic—Do we indeed live to see the day, when his and their pledges are to be disowned & trampled upon, and others, as worthless as they are delusive, offered in their stead? But the most odius and revolting feature in this business is yet to be mentioned. By another part of his talk, President Jackson would make it appear that at the very time that this plain, important and solemn guarantee, was entered into, there was a lurking article in the Constitution of the United States, something about the admission of new States, that annulled it— Good Heaven! Has not the blood of every American suffused his face and indignation fill his heart at such a suggestion?

President Jackson having, by a constitutional objection, shown his desire thus to put aside the guarantee of Washington, and bring us under the legislation of Georgia, which towards a free people like us, is perhaps as cruel as any in existence, proposes that Congress shall cede us a territory west of the Mississippi, "to be guaranteed to the Indian Tribes as long as they shall occupy it"—"where they may be secure in the enjoyment of government of their own choice, &c, &c."

Leaving out of view the confidence that could prompt to an offer of the pledge of General Jackson and the present Congress, in exchange for that of the Father of his Country and the Congress of Revolutionary Heroes—let us, as he has directed our attention to the Constitution, examine what authority he derives from it to offer to cede us a territory where we shall be independent. Well, I have examined this instrument—I can find there no such power—I say it cannot be found, or pointed out—it has no specific existence—Will it be asserted that it is a derivative power? —for the sake of consistency I would suppose not. For how can it be alleged that the tremendous power of ceding away the domain of the United States is implied. When it is denied that without specific power, the lands within the several States cannot be even improved by roads and canals with the money of the United States—and yet, with great Constitutional scruples on other points, the President calmly proposes to Congress to cede away the soil and sovereignty of the United States. I say of the United States for until it is theirs, they cannot give it to us.

Let those, who either through real or pretended humanity, would seek to have us removed to the western deserts, examine this matter—Let those religious associations in New York; who propose to second the views of State policy examine well the bearings of this matter. We are utterly lost, — there is not a shadow of hope for us if we part with our present lands.

But in addition to suggesting a lurking article in the Constitution as annulling the engagement of General Washington, President Jackson is pleased to sneer at our title to our country, in the following terms—-"But it seems to me visionary to suppose that in this state of things, claims can be allowed on tracts of country, on which they have never dwelt nor made improvements, merely because they have seen them from the mountain, or passed them in the chase." If this however, were our only title, it is superior to the less than nothingness of that title under which Georgia claims our country. She claims under what is called a Charter from a British King, who was never within three thousand miles of it—who never once saw our health invigorating mountains—who never quaffed our pure and crystal streams—who never experienced the luxury of our shady forests—or ever contemplated with mingled admiration and awe, as we have done, the wild majesty of Tallulla—or been sprinkled by the cooling spray of Tocoa—whose ignorance of this situation of our country is apparent on the very face of that Charter.

And who is it that thus sneers at our title, and under that sneer would do away the guarantee of Washington? It is that General Jackson by whose side our warriors poured forth their blood in the battle field—whose brows we assisted to bind with the only wreath that graces them, that of the warrior—whom a reference to the country and history of his forefathers, might have taught pity for us, from the wrongs of a people, who like ourselves, were calumniated that they might,without sympathy, be oppressed and despoiled. See by the following complaint, how closely their unhappy situation corresponded with our own. They state "that in 1170, Adrian had, at the unjust and iniquitous suggestion of Henry, King of England, by a certain verbal form, and without any legal and just process, deprived them of their domain, their people and country. The English sought under the external appearance of sanctity and religion, to extirpate the Irish nation. They drove them from their spacious habitations and paternal property, to dwell in woods, lakes, marshes & caverns, and sought to expel them even from these wretched places of refuge."

Leaving out of view our friendly reception of the first Georgians—our extensive grants of land to both their fathers and themselves—our relinquishing the friendly interference of other nations and putting ourselves under the protection of the United States—our having fought their battles—our treaty guarantees with them—who could have imagined, that at this day, when the monarchy of England has just enfranchised a long oppressed people—when the monarchy of France has just acknowledged the freedom of a revolted colony—at this day, when those who have been held as natural enemies are found leaguing together , to give freedom to an ancient nation—who could have imagined that at such a period,the head of this great Republic, would present the spectacle of offering to the most free and public spirited (but now weak) people on earth, the humiliating alternative of evil or slavery.[70]

70 *Cherokee Phoenix*, January 6, 1820. http://www.wcu.edu/library/DigitalCollections/CherokeePhoenix/Vol2/no39/pg1col5cpg2col2b.htm

Cherokee Law

As recorded by John Ridge,
Secretary to the Cherokee Nation

Whereas a Law has been in existence for many years, but not committed to writing, that if any citizen or citizens of this nation should treat and dispose of any lands belonging to this nation without special permission from the national authorities, he or they shall suffer death; — therefore, resolved, by the Committee and Council, in General Council convened, that any person or persons who shall, contrary to the will and consent of the legislative council of this nation in general council convened, enter into a treaty with any commissioner or commissioners of the United States, or any officers instructed for the purpose, and agree to sell or dispose of any part or portion of the national lands defined in the constitution of this nation, he or they so offending, upon conviction before any of the circuit judges of the Supreme Court, shall suffer death... Be it further resolved, that any person of persons, who shall violate the provisions of this act, and shall refuse, by resistance, to appear at the place designated for trial, or abscond, are hereby declared to be outlaws; and any person or persons, citizens of this nation, may kill him or them so offending, in any manner most convenient, within the limits of this nation, and shall not be held accountable for the same.[71]

---

71 *Laws of the Cherokee Nation*, from a facsimile of the 1852 edition (New York: Legal Classics Library).
http://www.commonlaw.com/home/legal-history-and-philosophy/laws-of-the-cherokee-nation

Anonymous

"The Indian and the White Man"

Cherokee Phoenix

January 20, 1830

When Gen. Lincoln went to make peace with the Creek Indians, one of the Chiefs asked him to sit down on a log. He did so. The chief then asked him to move, and in a few moments to move farther; the request was repeated till the General got to the end of the log; but the Chief still said, "Move farther;" to which the General replied," I can move no farther." "Just so it is with us," said the Chief…[72]

72 *Cherokee Phoenix*, January 20, 1830. http://www.wcu.edu/library/DigitalCollections/CherokeePhoenix/Vol2/no40/pg2col4c-5a.htm

David Meriwether

Georgia state legislator and US. Congressman

We want the Cherokee lands in Georgia, but the Cherokees will not consent to cede them.[73]

73 Charles C. Royce, *The Cherokee Nation of Indians* (Washington: Smithsonian Institution Press, 1975), 175 https://archive.org/stream/chroniclesofokla30190okla/chroniclesofokla30190okla_djvu.txt

Andrew Jackson

US. President

In response to Meriwether's inquiry

You must get clear of them (the Cherokees) by legislation. Take judicial jurisdiction over their country; build fires around them, and do indirectly what you cannot effect directly.[74]

---

74 Ibid.

Elias Boudinot

Cherokee Phoenix and Indians' Advocate

December 16, 1829

"SAVAGE HOSTILITIES"

Three eruptions have lately been made into the nation by parties of whites from Georgia, which we will denominate savage hostilities. After many false alarms have been given of Indian hostilities and Indian wars, what will the public think of the following, for the truth of which we stand pledged. A party of whitemen eight in number, well armed with guns, in the dead of night, a few days since, came into Hightower, and forcibly entering a house, kidnapped three negroes; two of whom were free, and made their escape into Georgia. Another party, also well armed, came over to arrest "thirteen Cherokee Indians," for punishing a notorious thief. We refer our readers to the letter of George Saunders, and the affidavit of the thief, published in our last. At the same time another party from Habersham County, fifteen in number, we believe, entered another part of the nation, with hostile intentions. After killing a hog, and robbing the Indians, and doing other insufferable acts, some of the Cherokees showed signs of resistance, & demanded of the savage invaders, that they should make remuneration for the hog they had killed, and for other mischief they had done. They not being disposed to accede to this very reasonable demand, the Cherokees forcibly took one of their guns—after which they escaped into Georgia. This band of robbers will in all probability… have warrants issued against those Cherokees who have had the hardihood to stop their inequitous proceedings.[75]

---

75 *Cherokee Phoenix*, December 16, 1829 . http://www.wcu.edu/library/DigitalCollections/CherokeePhoenix/Vol2/no36/pg3col2a.htm

Elias Boudinot

Cherokee Phoenix

Wednesday, February 10, 1830

FIRST BLOOD SHED BY THE GEORGIANS!!

...We have been told by a gentleman who passed this place as an express to the agent, from the principal chief, that a Cherokee has, at last, been killed by the intruders, and three more taken bound into Georgia! We are not prepared this week to give the public any particulars respecting this unpleasant affair. The general facts are, however, these, the particulars of which will be given in our next. A company of Cherokees, among whom were some of our most respectable citizens, constrained by the repeated aggressions and insults of a number of intruders, who had settled themselves far in the country, & likewise by the frequent losses sustained by many of our citizens in cattle and horses from their own countrymen, who are leagued in wickedness with our civilized brothers, started the other day, under the authority of the Principal Chief to correct, at least part of the evil. They were out two days, in which time they arrested four Cherokee horse-thieves. These received exemplary punishment. They found also 17 families of intruders, living, we believe, in Cherokee houses. These they ordered out and after safely taking out their beddings, chairs, &c. the houses were set on fire. In no instance was the least violence used on the part of the Cherokees. When the company returned home, five of them tarried on the way, who, we are sorry to say, had become intoxicated. In this situation, they were found by a company of intruders, twenty five in number. —One was killed, & three taken into Georgia.

Thus a circumstance, which we have for a long time dreaded, and which has been brought about by the neglect of the executive to remove the great nuisance to the Cherokees, has happened. We are nevertheless glad that the injury received is on the side of this nation. It has been the desire of our enemies that the Cherokees may be urged to some desperate act—thus far this desire has never been realized, and we hope, notwithstanding the great injury now sustained, their wanted forbearance will be continued. If our word will have any weight with our countrymen in this very trying time, we would say: forbear, forbear—revenge not, but leave vengeance to him "to whom vengeance belongeth."

P. S. On last Saturday, it was reported, that a large company of Georgians were on their way to arrest Mr. Ross and Major Ridge. We think it not improbable that an attempt of that kind will be made. If so, self defence, on the part of the Cherokees, many of whom , we understand, were at Ross's and Ridge's would undoubtedly be justifiable.[76]

76 *Cherokee Phoenix*, February 10, 1830. http://www.wcu.edu/library/DigitalCollections/CherokeePhoenix/Vol2/no43/pg2col4-5b.htm

John Ross

Chief of the Cherokee Nation

Cherokee Phoenix

Head of Coosa (Rome, Georgia)

February 13, 1830

...With the view of preventing erroneous impressions from growing out of the various reports which will no doubt be circulated, respecting the late occurrences with the intruders, I deem it my duty to make a true statement of facts.

It is generally known that there are divers intruders on Cherokee land, on the frontiers of the adjoining States, some of them being men of the most infamous character, and that the General Council at its last session made it my duty to remove such of them as may be found amidst our citizens in possession of the improvements recently abandoned by the Cherokees, who have emigrated to the Arkansas; and having been strongly urged by our good citizens to enforce said law, with the view of securing tranquility & the safety of their property, I complied with the request, without intending to disregard or interfere in the least degree with the instructions of the Secretary of War to the Agent. Therefore on the 4th instant, Major Ridge and other citizens were authorized & instructed to extend towards them all possible lenity and humanity. The men were prohibited from using ardent spirits whilst on duty. The intruders living on the public road leading to Alabama and at Saunders' old place were turned out of doors with all their effects. The company were fully persuaded that if the houses were not destroyed the intruders would not go away; they therefore determined on the expediency of setting fire to them. There were eighteen families of intruders thus removed, and having executed this duty with the utmost lenity towards them, and not having injured any of their property, the Cherokees felt no uneasiness, or alarm from any quarter, and returned home in small detached parties. Unfortunately, four of them became intoxicated and remained at Samuel Rowe's house where there was whiskey. In the course of the night of the 5th inst. a party of intruders, upwards of twenty men, armed with guns, came and arrested them; that is, The Waggon, Daniel Mills, Rattling

Gourd, and Chuwoyee. The first named was found in strings by the intruders, the Indians having tied him to prevent him from doing injury, and the second was beaten with a gun and stampled by the intruders, and the third was not hurt, but the fourth, who was unable to walk (being very drunk) was tied and put upon a horse, but not being able to sit on, and falling off once or twice, he was most barbarously beaten with guns &c. in the head, face, breast and arms, and was then thrown across the pummel of a saddle on a horse, and carried by the rider in that situation about one mile and then thrown off. The poor unfortunate man died the next morning and his corpse was left on the ground without any person to take care of it. The other three were sent into Carroll County, Georgia, under a guard.

As soon as I received intelligence of this unhappy affair, and understanding that the lawless intruders had threatened to kill Major Ridge and myself, and to burn our dwellings, I despatched an express to the Agent with all possible speed, demanding the arrest and punishment of the murderers, and the restoration of the prisoners, and also requesting the immediate interposition of his authority in preserving peace and harmony on the frontier. On the 7th I despatched a small waggon after the corpse of the murdered man, and on the 8th he was decently buried at his own house by the side of the graves of his father and mother. The corpse was shockingly mangled. Without reflection, after the burial, a platoon of small arms was fired, and heard a number of miles off, which alarmed the people, and led them to suspect that the intruders had attacked us; this caused messengers forthwith to run from Turnip Mountain in various directions. In the course of that night and the following day, a number of men came in to ascertain the fact. In the meantime, The Waggon & Daniel Mills, two of the prisoners who were taken into Carrol County, returned, having made their escape from the guard, when within a few miles of Carrollton. The Wagon received a severe stab in the breast with a butcher knife, and a cut across his left wrist, from the hands of the notorious Old Philpot. The Cherokees who had thus collected here from the false alarm were advised with the utmost earnestness to remain peaceably and quietly at their homes, and to remove all fears, and not to seek or attempt any private revenge for the death of their

Countryman, as the interposition of the United States agents authority was called for and expected.

On the evening of the 10th, the sub agent, Col. Williams arrived under instructions from the agent, and a few hours thereafter, a messenger arrived from Turnip Mountain with intelligence that a party of armed mounted white men had made descent upon Mr. Chas. Vann. Mr. West, his son Ezekiel, Charles Fields, one or two other Cherokees who happened at the same time to be there. When this band were seen in full speed coming up the lane, swearing and yelling in the most savage manner, it was proposed by Mr. Vann to his friends that they should get out of the way; consequently himself and the two Mr. Wests mounted their horses, (the others entered into an adjacent thicket), and in galloping up the road near Tally›s place, Mr. West was fired upon; he then dismounted his horse and returned the fire; fortunately, there was no execution done. As soon as this was heard at Turnip Mountain, messengers were immediately sent from there in various directions, presuming that Major Ridge and I would also be attacked. In the course of that night several Cherokees came in, and the next morning Col. Williams determined to pursue the party who had fired on Mr. West, with the view of endeavoring to prevent any farther attempt of disturbing the peace and harmony of the Cherokees. Being convinced from the expresses which I understood had been sent from Turnip Mountain, that a great many men from various places would soon come in, I suggested to Col. Williams the propriety of keeping them together until he was heard from. I recommended this course with the view of preventing further alarms, and if compulsion required, to act defensively, and that on their retirement, such man may be prepared to state facts for the satisfaction of the people.

I have since been informed that the Sheriff of Carroll County was at the head of the band who fired on Mr. West, and that when Mr. West returned the fire, they made a sudden halt and turned back to the Turnpike gate.- In the course of that night Messrs. David Vann and Daniel Griffin revisited them, and had some conversation with the Sheriff, who had a number of warrants for the arrest of the persons and property of those Cherokees who were engaged in removing the intruders and burning the Indians› houses occupied by them. Upon being prevailed upon, the Sheriff agreed that if Messrs. Vann and Griffin would go with him, and two or three of his men, he would in the morning come over to see me. This was agreed upon, but as soon as Mr. Vann returned home, the Sheriff and his men decamped with all possible haste for Carroll County. It is also stated that the number of armed men who escorted the Sheriff was about 25. The most of them were intruders upon Cherokee lands and of debased character, and that some of them were also accessary to the murder of Chuwoyee.

If it is thus that the laws of Georgia are to be extended and executed over the Cherokees, it is very obvious that justice and humanity are not to be respected. The very occurrences of these illegal and vicious proceedings testify to the fact in columns not to be mistaken, because a part of the very intruders who were peaceably removed by the Cherokees are said to be men of such vile character as could not live under their own laws even in Carroll County. Agreeably to treaty stipulation, which is the supreme law of the land, these very men, by their own acts, had forfeited the protection of the United States, and had made themselves liable to be punished by the Cherokees or not as they please. Is it not strange and unaccountable that they should be protected by the laws of Georgia, when they commit outrageous acts upon the peaceable and inoffensive Cherokees, upon whose lands they have intruded?

The Cherokees have no intention of seeking or attempting private or public revenge for the murder of one of their inoffensive citizens, but they will patiently wait for justice through the proper tribunal.[77]

---

77 *Cherokee Phoenix*, February 17. 1830. http://www.wcu.edu/library/DigitalCollections/CherokeePhoenix/Vol2/no44/pg2col5b-pg3col2b.htm

The Indian Removal Act

May 28, 1830

An Act to provide for an exchange of lands with the Indians residing in any of the states or territories, and for their removal west of the river Mississippi.

Be it enacted by the Senate and House of Representatives of the United States of America, in Congress assembled, That it shall and may be lawful for the President of the United States to cause so much of any territory belonging to the United States, west of the river Mississippi, not included in any state or organized territory, and to which the Indian title has been extinguished, as he may judge necessary, to be divided into a suitable number of districts, for the reception of such tribes or nations of Indians as may choose to exchange the lands where they now reside, and remove there; and to cause each of said districts to be so described by natural or artificial marks, as to be easily distinguished from every other.

And be it further enacted, That it shall and may be lawful for the President to exchange any or all of such districts, so to be laid off and described, with any tribe or nation of Indians now residing within the limits of any of the states or territories, and with which the United States have existing treaties, for the whole or any part or portion of the territory claimed and occupied by such tribe or nation, within the bounds of any one or more of the states or territories, where the land claimed and occupied by the Indians, is owned by the United States, or the United States are bound to the state within which it lies to extinguish the Indian claim thereto.

And be it further enacted, That in the making of any such exchange or exchanges, it shall and may be lawful for the President solemnly to assure the tribe or nation with which the exchange is made, that the United States will forever secure and guaranty to them, and their heirs or successors, the country so exchanged with them; and if they prefer it, that the United States will cause a patent or grant to be made and executed to them for the same: Provided always, That such lands shall revert to the United States, if the Indians become extinct, or abandon the same.

And be it further enacted, That if, upon any of the lands now occupied by the Indians, and to be exchanged for, there should be such improvements as add value to the land claimed by any individual or individuals of such tribes or nations, it shall and may be lawful for the President to cause such value to be ascertained by appraisement or otherwise, and to cause such ascertained value to be paid to the person or persons rightfully claiming such improvements. And upon the payment of such valuation, the improvements so valued and paid for, shall pass to the United States, and possession shall not afterwards be permitted to any of the same tribe.

And be it further enacted, That upon the making of any such exchange as is contemplated by this act, it shall and may be lawful for the President to cause such aid and assistance to be furnished to the emigrants as may be necessary and proper to enable them to remove to, and settle in, the country for which they may have exchanged; and also, to give them such aid and assistance as may be necessary for their support and subsistence for the first year after their removal.

And be it further enacted, That it shall and may be lawful for the President to cause such tribe or nation to be protected, at their new residence, against all interruption or disturbance from any other tribe or nation of Indians, or from any other person or persons whatever.

And be it further enacted, That it shall and may be lawful for the President to have the same superintendence and care over any tribe or nation in the country to which they may remove, as contemplated by this act, that he is now authorized to have over them at their present places of residence: Provided, That nothing in this act contained shall be construed as authorizing or directing the violation of any existing treaty between the United States and any of the Indian tribes.

And be it further enacted, That for the purpose of giving effect to the Provisions of this act, the sum of five hundred thousand dollars is hereby appropriated, to be paid out of any money in the treasury, not otherwise appropriated.[78]

---

78 https://www.loc.gov/rr/program/bib/ourdocs/Indian.html

Elias Boudinot

Cherokee Phoenix

May 29, 1830

Before the next number of our paper shall be issued, the first day of June, the day set apart by Georgia, for the extension of her assumed jurisdiction over the Cherokees, and the execution of her laws touching the Indians, will have arrived. The day is now at hand—the Cherokees have looked to it deliberately—they have anticipated its approach, but they are still here, on the land of their fathers. So conscious are they of their rights as a people they they have thought it not best to avoid the threatened operation ... by a precipitate flight to the western wilds. They are still here, but not to agree or consent to come under these laws. This they never will do—they have protested against the measure, and will always protest against it.

When the time comes that state laws are to be executed with rigor, as they no doubt will be, backed by the executive of the United States, and the late decision of the Senate, upon the reprobate Cherokees, we are unable to say what the effects will be. To us, the future is but darkness. One thing we know, there will be suffering. The Cherokees will be a prey to the cupidity of white men— every indignity and every oppression will be heaped upon them. They have already undergone much, when the time is merely in anticipation, —how will it be when full license is given to their oppressors?

We have heretofore related instances where this indignity and oppression have been perpetrated on individuals of this nation. Besides those we have mentioned the following may perhaps convey a proper light to the public on the conduct of civilized men towards savages: In the neighborhood of Tarrapin Creek, there lives a Creek man by the name of Hog, who, by his industrious habits, has been enabled to accumulate some property, consisting, chiefly of large stocks of horses and cattle. Living as he does near his white brothers, who are clamorous for the removal of the Indians, that they may not be harassed by savage neighbors, his best horses became the objects of much desire to some of them. By the precaution of the Hog and the constant watch he kept about his stables and lots, he was able to preserve these horses. Finding they could not steal them, we understand another expedient was resorted to lately by these members of the "Pony Club." Four whitemen came to this Indian's house, two of whom were armed with rifles. Finding the Hog alone with his wife, one of the men who was armed, proposed to buy his horse, and offered his gun for compensation. The Creek Indian refused to sell for such a trifle. The white man then proposed to exchange with the Indian. The offer was again rejected, the Indians' horse being greatly superior in value to the other. At this the white man observed he would have the horse, and proceeded towards the lot with a bridle. Hog's wife discovering the intention of these men followed, and in attempting to prevent them from catching the horse, was knocked down by the other armed man with a gun. She fell senseless to the ground. Hog ran into the horse lit, & by driving off the horses, & giving the alarm, prevented these robbers from accomplishing their design. The woman lay for some time apparently dead; but finally came to herself. We understand she is better, and is likely to recover.

Comment is unnecessary. We intreat you, respected reader,—we implore you, to pause after perusing the above facts, and reflect upon the effects of civilized legislation over poor savages. The laws which are the result of this legislation, are framed expressly against us, and not a clause in our favor. We cannot be a party or a witness in any of the courts where a white man is a party. Here is the secret. Full license to our oppressors, and every avenue of justice closed against us. Yes, this is the bitter cup prepared for us by a republican and religious Government—we shall drink it to the very dregs. [79]

---

79 *Cherokee Phoenix*, May 29, 1830. http://www.wcu.edu/library/DigitalCollections/CherokeePhoenix/Vol3/no06/3no06_p3-c1A.htm

Red Bird

Gwinnett County, Georgia

A letter to the Cherokee Phoenix

September 11, 1830

A few days ago, the Sheriff of Gwinnett County arrived at this place, with an old Cherokee Lady in his custody under close guard, whom he was taking to jail for debt. The Officer and his guard had another writ for one of our inhabitants. When they attempted to serve the writ, he made a retreat for some distance and then stopped.—In the meantime the Sheriff got his saddle bags from off his horse, and took from thence a pistol—he ran to get ahead of the criminal (for so it must be considered these republican days) who was then standing. The officer then came within a short distance and presented the pistol, and declared he would shoot him down if he attempted to escape. The next day they took him to jail for the enormous crime of being in debt. The old lady gave security and returned home.

This is as fair a statement of the affair as I can give, being an eye witness to a greater part of the transaction.

I should like Mr. Editor, if you or some of your readers, who are better acquainted with the laws of the State of Georgia than I am, would inform me through the medium of your paper, whether the officer of that state have the right, by law, to present a pistol or gun, and threaten to kill, in serving a civil writ, especially when there is no resistance.[80]

---

80 *Cherokee Phoenix*, September 4, 1830. http://www.wcu.edu/library/DigitalCollections/CherokeePhoenix/Vol3/no17/3no17_p2-c1A.htm

Elias Boudinot

An answer to Red Bird

Cherokee Phoenix

September 11, 1830

We are sorry we cannot satisfactorily answer the question of our correspondent. We know not what are, and what are not the laws of Georgia, having never sworn allegiance to them. We believe in other Governments it would have been unlawful for this Sheriff of Gwinnett County to do as he has done. We should hardly think that an officer was obliged to expose his life by threatening to kill, with a pistol in his hand, in every case of civil process. Be that as it may, everything is lawful with *tyranny and despotism*.[81]

---

81 Ibid.

Chostosa, John Wickliff, John Timson, Sweetwater, Sitaugi, and Kaneeda

Cherokee Phoenix and Indians' Advocate

September 11, 1830

To the citizens of the United States

Friends and brethren:

The occasion of our present address is one, which affects not only the well being, but the very existence of our country.

A course of policy has of late been pursued with relation to us, which we consider to be at variance with the most solemn treaties & which has filled our minds with painful anxiety.

Oppression is at this moment in vigorous operation under the appellation of laws of Georgia. These overbearing and cruel edicts are evidently designed to exterminate us from the earth. Under the sable banners of these pretended laws, are already marshalled for the purposes of rapine and plunder a host of the most abandoned characters who drive off our property, break the repose of our families, imprison our persons, and threaten our lives. But these laws grant us no hearing: they afford us no redress.

We consider these doings to be flagrant violations of those identical treaties by virtue of which millions of acres of land, ever ours are now vested in the United States as the price of protection against these very evils.

We have asked your Executive, for the stipulated protection: but it is not granted. We have petitioned Congress; but without success. We have assumed the attitude of abject suppliants, in soliciting that for which we have paid in full tale; but we have met nothing but mortifying repulses. We are grieved. We are oppressed. What are we to do, where shall we look for succor? The arm of your President heretofore potent to enforce justice has lost its wanted energy; he cannot help us.

The State of Georgia, in the vehemence of her thirst for sovereignty, has overleaned her bounds. She tramples on our dearest rights and frowns to silence the interrogators of justice.

People of America, where shall we look? Republicans we appeal to you. Christians we appeal to you. We need the exertion of your strong arm, we need the utterance of your commanding voice, we need the aid of your prevailing prayers.

In times past, your compassions, yearned over our moral desolation, and the misery which was spreading among us though the failure of game our ancient resource. The cry of wretchedness reached your hearts; you supplied us with implements of husbandry, and domestic industry, which enabled us to provide food and clothing for ourselves.—You sent us instructions in letters and the true religion which has chased away much of our mental and moral darkness.

Your wise President Jefferson took much pains to instruct us in the science of civilized government and recommended the government of the United States and of the several states as models for our imitation. He urged us also to industry and the acquisition of property. His letter was read in our towns; and we received it as the counsel of a friend. We commenced learning. We commenced improving our government. And by gradual advances we have attained our present station. But our venerable father Jefferson never intended that whenever we should arrive at a certain point in the science of government, of the knowledge of civilized arts, that our rights would be forfeited, our treaties become obsolete, the protection guaranteed them withdrawn, our property confiscated to lawless banditti, and our necks placed under the foot of Georgia.

If your benevolence responded to our silent petitions where we possessed no other claims than our wretchedness, and no other advocate than generous emotions of your own breasts, we feel assured that our appeal will not be disavowed when we ask for justice at your hands.

Much industry has been employed to misrepresent our condition, our faults, and our misfortunes and our defects have been magnified; and unfounded odium has been cast upon our name as if the worthlessness of our character and the degradation of our condition could exonerate the United States government from her engagements and annul the binding force of the treaties.

Sometimes our untamable barbarism and deplorable degradation are urged against us; and at others our civilization and our cultivation of domestic and social advances resulting therefrom are charged against us as unpardonable crimes.

It has been frequently asserted that we are willing and even desirous to go to the west. We assure our friends it is not so. We have our homes, we have our families, we love to dwell by our father's graves. We love to think that this land is our Great Creator's gift to them that he had permitted us to enjoy it after them and that our offspring are preparing to succeed us in the inheritance.

This land is our last refuge and it is our own. Our title to it has no defect, but the inferiority of our physical force, this defect is amply supplied by our compacts with the powerful and magnanimous government of the United States.

Respected and honored friends, permit us to speak plainly. Much has been done against us. Promises, threats, and stratagems have been employed. But we are still unshaken in our attachment to the land of our birth, and we do sollemnly protest against the exercise of oppressive measures to effect our removal. We protest against the extention of the laws of Georgia over any part of our territory; against the occupancy of our lands by U.S. citizens in virtue of compacts between the U. S. government and another nation with which we have no political connection and which possesses no rights within our territory against the removal of our boundary lines; and against the employment of money or other bribes to corrupt our citizens and induce them to become traitors to their country; and against the distribution of our annuities amongst individuals as being all contrary to the letter and spirit of our treaties.

We are greatly encouraged in bearing up under accumulated wrongs, to know that our rights are acknowledged and our claims advocated by a great majority of the wise, the honorable, and the virtuous among the citizens of the United States.

Brethren, while we beg your acceptance of the imperfect expression of our unfeigned gratitude for your past exertions, we ask with the most earnest solicitude of respect, the continuance of your aid in every way which your wisdom and philanthropy may dictate. And trusting to the … dance of all wise Providence; we are encouraged to look forward through generations yet to come, in the hope that the Cherokees will be still known on their native soil; that the light of truth which already illuminated our horizon will advance to meridian splendor, and that the magnanimous deeds of the vindicators of our rights will live in the memory and the veneration of our posterity long after our bodies shall have mingled with the dust.[82]

---

82 *Cherokee Phoenix*, September 11, 1830. http://www.wcu.edu/library/DigitalCollections/CherokeePhoenix/Vol3/no18/3no18_p2-c5A.htm

George R. Gilmer

Georgia governor

A letter to Andrew Jackson

June 20, 1831

It is important that the Government of the State should know whether it has become impossible for the United States to execute the contract of 1802, so that its policy in relation to the Cherokees may no longer be influenced by the expectation of that event.

...The State must put an end to even the semblance of a distinct political society among them.

....The millions of acres of land which are now of no value, except to add to the gratification of the idle ambition of the chiefs, must be placed in the possession of actual cultivators of the soil, who may be made the instruments for the proper administration of the laws.[83]

---

83 Document 512, *Correspondence on the Subject of the Emigration of Indians*, Nov. 1831-Dec. 133 (Washington: Duff Green, 1835), 481.

John W. West

Cherokee Nation citizen

Beaver Ponds

(near current Cave Spring, GA)

1831

I was dispossessed of (my home and property) located at the Beaver Ponds in the Cherokees East, by an act of the Legislature of the State of Georgia dated 1831. This act authorized the agents of Georgia to rent all improvements not immediately occupied by the Cherokees, by which act I was dispossessed and the premises taken from me, to my great loss. These proceedings of Georgia were previous to the Treaty of 1835.[84]

---

84 Marybelle W. Chase, *1842 Cherokee Claims, Saline District*, Claim No. 157 (from originals located at the Tennessee State Library and Archives, Nashville, Tennessee), 166-167.

Daniel S. Butrick

Missionary to the Cherokee Nation

From his journal

They were ... forbidden employing any white man to assist them, and by doing so, must forfeit the whole of their improvements.

Now as the Cherokees had long been in the habit of showing kindness to white people, especially to strangers, they could not at once overcome the current of their own feelings, so that when a white man came along with his family, and pleaded necessity and wished to labour only a few days, to get something to carry them on their journey, the Cherokees could not readily turn him away. And after being employed in this manner, this stranger would sometimes, it is said, take the advantage of the law and rob his benefactor of the farm he had been hired to work...

Br. George Hicks..., a very industrious and honest Indian, who had long been a worthy member of the United Brethren's church, had had for some time a white man in his family whom he had obliged with a home as he had none of his own. This man he did not immediately drive from his house, on the passage of the above law, and on that account was himself driven with his family into the woods. The weather was wet and cold, and the ground covered with snow, when a white man came to his house, and ordered him to take away all his furniture, etc. as he wanted the house. Mr. Hicks told him that rather than take his family out doors during such weather, he would give him two dollars per day, if his family could remain in the house till he could find some place to put them.

But this could not be granted; and the man commenced fetching his own furniture into the house. The house was built of hewn logs, and had a good roof, good floors, etc... There was also some valuable furniture in it. One cupboard especially which cost $25, chairs, table etc. These Mr. Hicks had to remove, and eventually most were lost.

The man also ordered him to take away his creatures, and clear his corn cribs, as he wanted them. Mr. Hicks was therefore obliged to take his family into the woods, when he found an old sugar camp, into which he crowded his bed etc, till he could obtain assistance to move to Mr. Clauders on Connessauga... [85]

85 Daniel S. Butrick, *The Journal of Rev. Daniel S. Butrick, May 19, 1838 – April 1, 1839* (Park Hill: The Trail of Tears Association, Oklahoma Chapter, 1998), 16.

John Ross & Others

Chief of the Cherokee Nation

From a Memorial presented to US. Congress

Relation of the dispossession of Joseph Vann

Mr. Joseph Vann, … a native Cherokee, was a man of great wealth, had about eight hundred acres of land in cultivation; had made extensive improvements, consisting, in part, of a brick house, costing about ten thousand dollars, mills, kitchens, negro houses, and other buildings. He had fine gardens, and extensive apple and peach orchards. His business was so extensive, he was compelled to employ an overseer and other agents. In the fall of 1833, he was called from home, but before leaving, made a conditional contract with a Mr. Howell, a white man, to oversee for him in the year 1834, to commence on the first of January of that year. He returned about the 28th or 29th of December 1833, and learning Georgia had prohibited any Cherokee from hiring a white man, told Mr. Howell he did not want his services. Yet Mr. (William) Bishop, the state's agent, represented to the authorities of Georgia, that Mr. Vann had violated the laws of that State, by hiring a white man, had forfeited his right of occupancy, and that a grant ought to issue for his lands. There were conflicting claims under Georgia for his possessions. A Mr. Riley pretended a claim, and took possession of the upper part of the dwelling house, armed for battle. Mr. Bishop … and his party came to take possession, and between them and Riley, a fight commenced, and from twenty to fifty guns were fired in the house. While this was going on, Mr. Vann gathered his trembling wife and children into a room for safety. Riley could not be dislodged from his position up stairs, even after being wounded, and Bishop's party finally set fire to the house. Riley surrendered and the fire was extinguished.

Mr. Vann and his family were then driven out, unprepared, in the dead of winter, and snow upon the ground, through which they were compelled to wade, and take shelter within the limits of Tennessee, in an open log cabin, upon a dirt floor, and Bishop put his brother Absalom in possession of Mr. Vann's house. This Mr. Vann is the same, who, when a boy, volunteered as a private soldier in the Cherokee regiment, in the service of the United States, in the Creek war, periled his life in crossing the river at the battle of the Horse Shoe. What has been his reward?[86]

86 *Memorial Protest of the Cherokee Nation, 1836*. United States Congressional Serial Set, House Document 286, 24th Congress, 1st session.

Eli Scott

Chatoga District

Feb. 15, 1832

My mare and hogs were stolen from me on the 15th February 1832 by four white men whose names I do not know. I was informed by Oo Wo Sa Hee a Cherokee man that he had seen four white men driving my hogs and that one of the men rideing (one) of my mares. Oo Wo Sa Hee was acquainted with my stock as he knew them & then persued after the men and traced them for about five miles in the direction of Carroll County, Georgia and then turned back home as the men was then about two days ahead of me and it was important for me to overtake them before they would cross the line with the hogs. And my cows & calves was also stolen from me in the Spring of 1832. I traced them about 12 miles as far as Cedar Town in Old Nation. Then I saw a man that gave me a discription of my cattle. He said that he had seen two white men driving these cows & calves by his house in the direction of Carroll County Geo. And I have good reason to think from the discription that they were the same cattle that I had lost and that white men had stolen them from me. I have never heard of my property since.[87]

87 Marybelle W. Chase, *1842 Cherokee Claims, Goingsnake District,* Claim No. 25 (from originals located at the Tennessee State Library and Archives, Nashville, Tennessee), 34.

Martin Downing

A claim for two horses

The claimant in this case states (on oath) that the whites stole the horses charge in the account (2 horses $130) from him forcibly in his sight & that his situation was such among the whites his evidence would do him no good.[88]

88 Marybelle W. Chase, *1842 Cherokee Claims, Saline District*, Claim No. 193 (from originals located at the Tennessee State Library and Archives, Nashville, Tennessee), 196.

Daniel S. Butrick

A missionary

At Cassville, it is said, some poor Cherokees were enticed to drink, and when drunk, one of the women was taken out into the public street, and her clothes pulled up, and tied over her head, and thus she was left to the gaze of the multitudes passing by.

Again, an aged Cherokee woman went to that vile town on business with her grand daughter, and grand son. On leaving the village, it is said, they were followed by two young men and after they had proceeded some distance, the men overtook them, seized the young woman, pulled her from her horse, as she sat behind her younger brother, drawing their knives at the same time to keep the brother and grandmother from them.

They drew the young woman some distance from the road, and while one was abusing her in the most shameful manner, the other was fighting away her almost frantic grandmother & brother.

After abusing her in this manner as long as they wished, they took her to a vacant house near by and frightened her friends away, and it was not, I believe, till the next day, that she was permitted to wander, in shame, to her home.

...(T)he Indians, being considered savages, were denied the oath (in a court of law), and of course must submit to whatever abuse was heaped upon them.[89]

89 Daniel S. Butrick, *The Journal of Rev. Daniel S. Butrick, May 19, 1838 – April 1, 1839* (Park Hill: The Trail of Tears Association, Oklahoma Chapter, 1998), 14.

John Marshall

Chief Justice, US. Supreme Court

From the majority opinion

Worcester v. Georgia

1832

...From the commencement of our government, Congress has passed acts to regulate trade and intercourse with the Indians; which treat them as nations... All these acts ... manifestly consider the several Indian nations as distinct political communities, having territorial boundaries, within which their authority is exclusive, and having a right to all the lands within those boundaries, which is not only acknowledged, but guaranteed by the United States…

The Indian nations had always been considered as distinct, independent political communities, retaining their original natural rights, as the undisputed possessors of the soil, from time immemorial ... The very term nation so generally applied to them, means 'a people distinct from others.'

... The Cherokee nation, then, is a distinct community, occupying its own territory, in which the laws of Georgia can have no force, and which the citizens of Georgia have no right to enter, but with the assent of the Cherokees themselves, or in conformity with treaties, and with the acts of congress.[90]

---

90 *Niles' Weekly Register*, Vol. 42, 56. http://www.wwnorton.com/college/history/foner2/contents/common/documents/ch10_1832_2_transcript.htm

John Ridge

A letter to cousin Stand Watie from Washington City

April 6, 1832

...That it has been a day of rejoicing with patriots of our Country on hearing of the glorious decision of the Supreme Court, I can readily perceive and congratulate them upon the momentous event. But you are aware and ought to advise our people that the contest is not over and that time is to settle the matter either for us and all the friends of the Judiciary or against us all! We have gained a high standing and consideration in the interests and best affections of the community from which we can never be removed. But Sir, the Chicken Snake General Jackson has time to crawl and hide in the luxuriant grass of his nefarious hypocracy until his responsibility is fastened upon by an execution of the Supreme Court at their next session. Then we shall see how strong the links are to the chain that connect the states to the Federal Union. Upon this subject the Union pauses and stands still to look upon the crisis our intellectual warfare has brought them and the Cherokee question as it now stands is the greatest that has ever presented itself to the consideration of the American People. Upon the shoulders of this body politic, if there was a proper head, the friends of the permanency of the general government could look upon this decision undismayed as to the results of the menacing attitude which the foolish Georgians have assumed.

Now before the explained laws are carried into effect, it will, I fear, first be necessary to cut down this Snake's head and throw it down in the dust. From the newspaper editorial remarks, you will be afforded the opportunity to see the operations of this affair and the length of the rope that Georgia has to browse upon the rights of the Cherokee Nation. The remarks I have thought called for on this occasion, that we as a whole and individually, may not sleep upon our post, but as good soldiers watch thoroughly every avenue through which the enemy may approach.

The Secretary of War is exceedingly anxious to close a treaty with our Nation upon the basis that will secure to us the sovereignty and fee of and over the soil west of the Mississippi and money enough to make every friend to his country rich with the addition of a perpetual annuity for the support of public institutions. I feel disgusted at an administration who have trampled our rights under foot to offer new pledges from their rotten hearts. He says that Jack Walker and James Stark have informed him that there is a majority in favor of a treaty on the Tennessee side of the Cherokee Nation and that they believe they are also in the majority in the limits of North Carolina of this description. The Secretary says that if so, they will treat with them or any of the other bands who shall prove to be in the majority there. I told him that it was false and granting for the sake of argument that the Government succeeded in making a treaty with a fraction or faction of our Nation, he knew very well that it would never be ratified by the Senate constituted as it was, as we assuredly would protest against it and defeat it.

In view of these facts, have I not said well when I said you should be on your guard? As to the Arkansas delegation they can never do hurt and their greatest hope is to cling fast to our friendship and to reunite with us. If the time ever should happen to come when we thought best to make a treaty, we should do so. This is their language. Rest assured, dear Cousin, that we have the advantage and let this question result which way it may. As I have said before, we shall live to tread on the necks of traitors. It may well yet be a fearful time for them if they have hearts for reflection to know that they have only been false and done mischief to themselves....

From the strain of this letter, you will perceive that it is not for publication.

"United we stand, divided we fall." Since the decision of the Supreme Court, I have felt greatly revived – a new man and I feel independent. I am hoping you all do too. How much of gratitude do we owe to the good men Mr. Worcester and Dr. Butler. You did not mention my son, Rollin. Present my best respects to Mrs. W. and Mrs. B. and Miss Sawyer. I shall, you know, always be glad to hear from you...[91]

---

91 Edward Everett Dale and Gaston Litton, *Cherokee Cavaliers* (Norman: University of Oklahoma Press, 1939), 7-10.

Andrew Jackson

US. President

A letter to John Coffee

1832

...the decision of the Supreme Court has fell still born, and they find that they cannot coerce Georgia to yield to its mandate.[92]

92 Ronald N. Satz, *American Indian Policy in the Jacksonian Era* (Norman: University of Oklahoma Press, 1974), 49.

Jack Winn

Cherokee Nation citizen
Hickory Log District
1832

After the laws of Georgia were extended over the Cherokee Nation ...they also took my Turnpike Gate out of my possession in 1832. The road that the gate was on led from Tennessee to Georgia and … I never received any compensation for the same…[93]

93 Marybelle W. Chase, *1842 Cherokee Claims, Goingsnake District,* Claim No. 332 (from originals located at the Tennessee State Library and Archives, Nashville, Tennessee), 294.

Oowahistauahee

Cherokee Nation citizen

Chattooga Valley

I had in my possession ... houses, farm & fruit trees in the Old Nation and...in the year 1832 or 1833 I was turned out of my house by a white man who claimed the lot on sections of the land I resided on and in consequence of my Cherokee neighbors being also drove from their places (my) houses & farm was not known as a Cherokee improvement at the time the valuing agents were sent out through (the) Nation to value improvements and therefore I have lost the … items entirely.[94]

94 Marybelle W. Chase, *1842 Cherokee Claims, Flint District, Vol. 3,* Claim No. 106 (from originals located at the Tennessee State Library and Archives, Nashville, Tennessee), 327-328.

The Bread

Cherokee Nation citizen
High Tower River (Etowah River)
1833

In the year 1833 while working in the gold mine in Georgia I was seized, assaulted, and imprisoned, I not being aware at the time of any existing law prohibiting persons from working in said mine. [95]

---

95 Marybelle W. Chase, *1842 Cherokee Claims, Tahlequah District* (from originals located at the Tennessee State Library and Archives, Nashville, Tennessee), 171.

Kah-too

Cherokee Nation citizen

I was knocked down with a gun (by the Georgia Guard), the marks of which I carry on my head to this day, and also two pistols swiped for no other reason than digging gold in my own country and on my own land.[96]

96 Marybelle W. Chase, *1842 Cherokee Claims, Tahlequah District,* Claim No. 307 (from originals located at the Tennessee State Library and Archives, Nashville, Tennessee), 172.

Oowoteyohee

Cherokee Nation citizen

Alijah, Georgia (near modern Ellijay)

1833

In the year 1833...two horses....I have good reason to believe were stolen by (white) citizens, that they disappear and were followed into the white settlements but (I) could not get them and ...the corn and hogs and other articles charged were taken from me in the same year by a white man who claimed the lot of section of land I resided on. I was then compelled to move away and the said white man made use of all my hogs and corn and other articles...[97]

97 Marybelle W. Chase, *1842 Cherokee Claims, Flint District, Vol. 3,* Claim No. 113 (from originals located at the Tennessee State Library and Archives, Nashville, Tennessee), 346-348

Anonymous

May 18, 1833

At Ellijay an industrious Indian had by his steady habits improved his premises to be of considerable value, when it was drawn by one of the lottery gamblers in Georgia. The fortunate holder of the ticket applied to the governor for a grant, which was given him, on his assurance that there was no Indian occupant on it. The fortunate drawer gathered up his all, including some two or three pistols, and moved to the Cherokee country, loaded his pistols, entered the possession of Ootawlunsta, pointing one at him, and drove the innocent Cherokee from his well cultivated field and was without a home the last accounts we had.

The Cherokees are destined to suffer.[98]

98 *Cherokee Phoenix*, May 18, 1833
http://neptune3.galib.uga.edu/ssp/News/chrkphnx/18330518c.pdf

Aiky Walker

Cherokee Nation citizen

McLemore's Cove, Northwest Georgia

1836

When the land was drawed for, in Georgia, a white man drew the land where it was laid off, a man (named Ned Bark) lived a near neighbor, had a small improvement, he enrolled and emigrated in 1836. When Bark left his improvement, the land was laid off in a lot, and took our improvement inside of this lot. The "Drawer" then came and took possession of our place, and turned us out of doors. There was a small house on the place I occupied that for some time. I was never afterwards allowed to do, or raise anything on the place, until at last I was forced to leave the place to seek some place to raise something to subsist on and to maintain my family. I moved from McLemore's Cove to Ross's Landing…[99]

99 Marybelle W. Chase, *1842 Cherokee Claims, Skin Bayou District*, (from originals located at the Tennessee State Library and Archives, Nashville, Tennessee), 207-208.

Brice Martin

Cherokee Nation citizen

1835

For the rent of 50 acres of land for 2 years @ $3 per acre $300

1125 Bushels corn @ $1.00

1125 $1425.

The claimant in this case states (on oath) that he was ejected from his place by one Berry Atkinson in the fall of 1835 in pursuance of an act of the Legislature of the State of Georgia, making it lawful for its citizens to remove the Cherokees from the Georgia lands who had become reservees under former Treaties, and as this act extended to their descendants, the claimant was dispossessed, his Father having been a reservee under the Treaty of Calhoun. The corn charged in this account was taken from him by the said Atkinson, on the ground that the crop was made after the passage of the act above named.[100]

100 Marybelle W. Chase, *1842 Cherokee Claims, Saline District*, Claim No. 72 (from originals located at the Tennessee State Library and Archives, Nashville, Tennessee), 69.

Nancy and Alecy, daughters of Dick-es-sky

Hightower River

Hickory Log District

1836

The 27 Acres of land on Hightower River our father was dispossessed of it in in the year 1836 by a white man named Bart Baily a citizen of Cherokee Georgia. And our father never received any rent for the land for the two years that he lay out of the use of it. And all the ballance of our property as charged in 1838 our father was forced to abandon it in his lifetime in 1838 by the Authorities of the United States for which in his lifetime he never received any compensation...[101]

101 Marybelle W. Chase, *1842 Cherokee Claims, Goingsnake District,* (from originals located at the Tennessee State Library and Archives, Nashville, Tennessee), 37-38.

Johnson

A Creek man living in the Cherokee Nation

Sixes Town

Coosawattee District

...Property and cash.... was taken from me by the whites during the late Creek War. Myself and company wishing to be peaceable we sought refuge among the Cherokees. We left the Creek Nation and went to Sixes Town in the Cherokee Nation East and took up camps where we was met by a set of white men armed with guns. They took all the property that they could find in our possession and money, which said white men did ... and for what causes or purposes I do not know...[102]

102 Marybelle W. Chase, *1842 Cherokee Claims, Goingsnake District,* (from originals located at the Tennessee State Library and Archives, Nashville, Tennessee), 310-311.

John Rollin Ridge

A relation of his early life in the Cherokee Nation

I was born in the Cherokee Nation, East of the Mississippi River, on the 19th of March, 1827. My earliest recollections are of such things as are pleasing to childhood, the fondness of a kind father, and smiles of an affectionate mother. My father, the late John Ridge, as you know, was one of the Chiefs of his tribe, and son of the warrior and orator distinguished in Cherokee Councils and battles, who was known amongst the whites as Major Ridge, and amongst his own people as Ka-nun-ta-cla-ge. My father grew up till he was some twelve or fifteen years of age, as any untutored Indian, and he used well to remember the time when his greatest delight was to strip himself of his Indian costume, and with aboriginal cane-gig in hand, while away the long summer days in wading up and down creeks in search of crawfish. At the age which I have mentioned above, a missionary station sprang into existence, and Major Ridge sent his son John, who could not speak word of English, to school at this station, placing him under the instruction of a venerable Missionary named Gambol. Here here he learned rapidly, and in the course of a year acquired a sufficient knowledge of the white man's language to speak it quite fluently.

Major Ridge had now become fully impressed with the importance of civilization. He had built him a log-cabin, in imitation of the border-whites and opened him a farm. The Missionary, Gambol, told him of an institution built up in a distant land expressly for the education of Indian youths (Cornwall, Connecticut), and here he concluded to send his son. After hearing some stern advice from his father, with respect to the manner to which he should conduct himself amongst the 'pale-faces,' he departed for the Cornwall School in charge of a friendly Missionary. He remained there until his education was completed. During his attendance at this institution, he fell in love with a young white girl of the place, daughter of Mr. Northrup. His love was reciprocated. He returned home to see his father, gained his consent, through with much difficulty (for the old Major wished him to marry a chief's daughter amongst his own people), went back again to Cornwall, and shortly brought his "pale-faced" bride to the wild country of the Cherokees. In due course of time, I, John Rollin, came into the world. I was called by my grandfather 'Chees-quat-a-law-ny,' which, interpreted, means 'Yellow Bird.' Thus you have a knowledge of my parentage and how it happened that I am an Indian.

Things had now changed with the Cherokees. They had a written Constitution and laws. They had legislative halls, houses and farms, courts, and juries. The general mass, it is true, were ignorant, but happy under the administration of a few simple, just, and wholesome laws. Major Ridge had become wealthy by trading with the whites and by prudent management. He had built an elegant house on the banks of the 'Oos-te-nar-ly River,' on which now stands the thriving town of Rome, Georgia.

Many a time in my buoyant boyhood have I strayed along its summer-shaded shores in the light canoe over its swiftly-rolling bosom, and beneath its over-hanging willows. Alas for the beautiful scene! The Indian's form haunts it no more!

My father's residence was a few miles east of the 'Oos-te-nar-ly.' I remember it well! A large two-storied house, on a high hill crowned with a fine grove of oak and hickory, a large, clear spring at the foot of the hill, and an extensive farm stretching away down into the valley, with a fine orchard on the left. On another hill some two hundred yards distant, stood the schoolhouse, built at my father's expense, for the use of a Missionary, Miss Sophia Sawyer, who made her home with our family and taught my father's children, and all who chose to come for her instruction. I went to this school until I was ten years of age— which was in 1837. Then another change had come over the Cherokee Nation. A demon-spell had fallen upon it. The white man had become covetous of the soil. The unhappy Indian was driven from his house — not one, but thousands — and the white man's ploughshare turned up the acres which he had called his own. Wherever the Indian built his cabin, and planted his corn, there was the spot which the white man craved. Convicted on suspicion, they were sentenced to death by laws whose authority they could not acknowledge, and hanged on the white man's gallows. Oppression became intolerable, and forced by extreme necessity, they at last gave up their homes, yielded their beloved country to the rapacity of the Georgians, and wended their way in silence and in sorrow to the forests of the far west.[103]

103 John Rollin Ridge, *Poems* (San Francisco: Edward Bosqui & Co., 1868), 4-6.

John Ridge, Elias Boudinot, and approximately 50 others

From a council meeting at Running Waters held "on behalf of those ... who are desirous of removing west of the Mississippi."

November 28, 1834

... In the full time of this successful improvement (of Cherokee civilization) all... hopes of happiness have been blasted, in consequence of the extension, by force, of the jurisdiction of the States ....

In the midst of the painful feeling which the destruction of our Government creates in our bosoms, we also perceive, the same melancholy fate has attended the other aboriginal tribes. On this side of the Mississippi scarcely a solitary council fire blazes under the heavens.

It is well known that our applications to the President, Congress, and the Supreme Court, to interpose the United States authority in our behalf, have all proved fruitless, as well as that the decisions of the Supreme Court in behalf of individuals claiming the right of protection under the Cherokee laws and treaties, have been disregarded by the State of Georgia....

... now, our earliest friends have told us that it is in vain to hope for the restoration of our rights.

In view of all these circumstances, we have been compelled to the hard case of choosing an alternative... In the decision we have made on this subject, we have taken the unhappy condition of our people, as individuals, into consideration. It is not to be disguised that there are in existence two parties among our people, whose policies are the antipodes of each other. Since the suppression of our Government, no elections have been held among us... The party who hold the councils at Red Clay have kept themselves in perpetual office by a resolution enacted of themselves. They are willing to take an individual standing in the States, and become citizens. Heretofore, as you will perceive, in looking at the treaty of 1819, the leaders of this party have already received valuable reservations in fee simple.

They hold their councils in the chartered limits of Tennessee. The party which we represent are not in favor of taking reservations of land, and abandoning the political existence of the nation…

When we reflect upon the character of our people in general, their ignorance, weakness, and total incapacity to contend in competition with the white man for wealth, science, and fame; and when we reflect on the fearful odds against which we have to run our career, laws expressly made to discredit us as men, with no legal rights to the soil, and all the unrelenting prejudices against our language and color in full force, we must believe that the scheme of amalgamation with our oppressors is too horrid for a serious contemplation. ...If then, it is the opinion of Congress that the tide of white population and State jurisdiction, which is pressing upon us, cannot be restrained, it would be the greatest act of humanity to devise immediate measures to remove our people upon as liberal terms as the General Government can afford....[104]

104 W. Jeff Bishop, *Running Waters: Forgotten Cherokee Council Ground* (Report for the National Park Service, 2008), 20.

Mary Fields

Fourteen-year-old Cherokee student
at the Running Waters School
Eight miles northeast of Rome, Georgia
1836

I am going to school, to Miss S. Sawyer now. I have learned great deal more now, than all the schools I ever went to. The first time I ever went to school was at Dr. Butler's, the second time in Tennessee, the third at New Echota. This is the fourth school I am into now.

Yesterday morning one of the little school boys was hurt very badly. He was kicked by a mule on his forehead, so Miss Sawyer had to sew his skin. The little boy was very patient, while Miss S. was dressing it. He is better now, he has studied some today.

All the children are learning first, in this school. Miss S. is the best teacher, I ever went to school to. I have been to school to three teachers two besides Miss S. Some of the children cannot talk English, nor understand. I have two sisters that is not talk English much, but they understand all we say. Miss S. makes these children that cannot speak English stand up, & repeat some hymns after her, that learns them to speak plain. Once I could not speak a word of English. When I was about six or eight years old. I am now fourteen, and on my fifteenth year.

I interpret every night to the children, that cannot understand, about the bible which we read.

The court house at New Echota was very cool, but the white people took it away. There was another small house, in the town, & Miss Sawyer kept her school in that house, at Mr. Ridges is very cool and pleasant, the trees are thick all around it. It has a smooth plank floor, & a large fire place & five glass windows, two large ones and three are shut with a slide. Two swallows have made a nest in the chimney. Every morning when we wake, the birds are singing sweetly around the school house.

Betsey Adair, Eleanor Boudinot, Rollin Ridge & myself are studying Geography, & Geometry. We have been studying Arithmetic. We read the History of the United States, in the after noon, & spell. We have been reviewing our lessons, & we have not spell any this week. Next week we shall spell. Then it will be the last week the school will continue. Perhaps I shall never go to school any more. Father's family will go to Arkansaw this fall.[105]

105 Ibid., 155-156.

Rachel Smith

Student at the Running Waters School

At John Ridge's plantation

Eight miles northeast of Rome, Georgia

May 18, 1836

I have been at school here nearly five months to Miss (Sophia) Sawyer. I live about thirty miles from Running Waters. I suppose you have heard of Big-Cabin Smith, my father is his son. My proud father once lived just about two miles from the Missionary Station at Haweis. He has been turned out from his house by the white people. He was very sick when he was turned out from his house, and has been very sick ever since. He is not able to go outdoors. The last time I heard from him they said that he could not talk loud, only just whisper. He is a very old man. They do not expect he will live long.[106]

106 Ibid., 166.

Rachel Smith

Student

May 20, 1836

Yesterday I heard that my proud father was dead. He died at his daughter's house. He was a very wicked man only a few years ago. He was converted after he was a very old man. Hope he was gone to heaven.[107]

107 Ibid.

Daniel S. Butrick

Missionary

A man by the name of Big Cabin, who had been many years a chief or councellor was sick with the consumption, & ready to die. But in some way a white man got the advantage of him … and ordered him directly to leave his house. His friends entreated that he might remain till he died; but in vain. His children were obliged to make a litter and carry him 12 miles, where he lived but a short time. He was a member of the Presbyterian church. [108]

108 Daniel S. Butrick, *The Journal of Rev. Daniel S. Butrick, May 19, 1838 – April 1, 1839* (Park Hill: The Trail of Tears Association, Oklahoma Chapter, 1998), 16.

Rachel Smith

Student

May 29, 1836

Mr. (John) Ridge has been expecting to come home (from Washington) every week for a long time. He has been waiting for the treaty to be ratified. There they have been all Winter, and done nothing yet. Our people are suffering most of them with hunger, and a great many have been turned out of their houses since, and some put in prison for being accused of stealing. We heard for truth that two old Cherokee men died near New Echota for want of food.[109]

---

109 W. Jeff Bishop, *Running Waters: Forgotten Cherokee Council Ground* (Report for the National Park Service, 2008), 166-167.

Rachel Smith

Student

June 8, 1836

Monday Mrs. Ridge received a letter from Mr. Ridge. He said that the Cherokee treaty was ratified, and (they) that were hungry would be furnished with food. Now all the Cherokees are obliged to go to the West, and all those that wish to stay in this Country, have to obey the Georgia laws, if they do not they cannot stay.[110]

110 Ibid., 167.

Elizabeth N. Adair

Student at the Running Waters School

Nine years old

A poem quoted from her school primer

"The Bird's Nest"

June, 1836

What note of sorrow strikes my ear
Is it their mother thus distrest?
Ah yes and see their father dear
Flies round and round, to seek their nest.[111]

111 Ibid., 160.

Maj. William M. Davis

A letter to the Secretary of War

March 5, 1836

I conceive that my duty to the President, to yourself, and to my country, reluctantly compels me to make a statement of facts in relation to a meeting of a small number of Cherokees at New Echota last December who were met by Mr. Schermerhorn and articles of a general treaty entered into between them for the whole Cherokee Nation.

I should not interpose in the matter at all but I discover that you do not receive impartial information on the subject... I will not be silent when I see that you are about to be imposed on by a gross and base betrayal of the high trust reposed in Rev. J. F. Schermerhorn by you.

Sir, that paper... called a treaty is no treaty at all, because not sanctioned by the great body of the Cherokees and made without their participation or assent. I solemnly declare to you that upon its reference to the Cherokee people it would be instantly rejected by nine-tenths of them and I believe by nineteen-twentieths of them. There were not present at the conclusion of the treaty more than one hundred Cherokee voters ... The most cunning and artful means were resorted to to conceal the paucity of numbers present at the treaty. No enumeration of them was made by Shermerhorn. The business of making the treaty was transacted with a committee appointed by the Indians present, so as not to expose their numbers.... The delegation ... had no more authority to make a treaty than any other dozen Cherokees accidentally picked up for that purpose.[112]

112 Vicki Rozema, *Voices from the Trail of Tears* (Winston-Salem: John F. Blair, 2003), 63-64

John Ross & Others

From a Memorial presented to US. Congress Head of Coosa (now Rome, Georgia)

1836

Mr. John Ross, the principal chief of the Cherokee Nation … was at Washington City, on the business of his nation. When he returned, he traveled until about 10 o'clock at night to reach his family; rode up to the gate; saw a servant believed to be his own; dismounted, ordered his horse taken; went in, and to his utter astonishment found himself a stranger in his own home, his family having been some days before driven out to seek a new home.

A thought then flitted across his mind — that he could not, under all the circumstances of the situation, reconcile it to himself to tarry all night under the roof of his own house as a stranger, the new host of that house being the tenant of that mercenary band of Georgia speculators at whose instance his helpless family had been turned out and made homeless.

Upon reflecting, however, that 'man is born unto trouble,' Mr. Ross at once concluded to take up his lodgings there for the night, and to console himself under the conviction of having met his afflictions and trials in a manner consistent with every principle of moral obligation towards himself and family, his country and his God.

On the next morning he arose early, and went out into the yard, and saw some straggling herds of his cattle and sheep browsing about the place — his crop of corn undisposed of. In casting a look up into the widespread branches of a majestic oak, standing within the enclosure of the garden, and which overshadows the spot where lie the remains of his dear babe and most beloved and affectionate father, he there saw, perched upon its boughs, that flock of beautiful pea-fowls, once the matron's care and delight, but now left to destruction and never more to be seen.

He ordered his horse, paid his bill, and departed in search of his family. After traveling amid heavy rains he had the happiness of overtaking them on the road, bound for some place of refuge within the limits of Tennessee. Thus have his houses, farm, public ferries, and other property been wrested from him. [113]

113 George Macgruder Battey Jr., *A History of Rome and Floyd County* (Marietta: Cherokee Publishing Company, 1922), 221-222. Also see: *Memorial Protest of the Cherokee Nation, 1836*. United States Congressional Serial Set, House Document 286, 24th Congress, 1st session.

John Ross

Chief of the Cherokee Nation

A letter written in 1836

It is well known that for a number of years past we have been harassed by a series of vexations, which it is deemed unnecessary to recite in detail, but the evidence of which our delegation will be prepared to furnish. With a view to bringing our troubles to a close, a delegation was appointed on the 23rd of October, 1835, by the General Council of the nation, clothed with full powers to enter into arrangements with the Government of the United States, for the final adjustment of all our existing difficulties. The delegation failing to effect an arrangement with the United States commissioner, then in the nation, proceeded, agreeably to their instructions in that case, to Washington City, for the purpose of negotiating a treaty with the authorities of the United States.

After the departure of the Delegation, a contract was made by the Rev. John F. Schermerhorn, and certain individual Cherokees, purporting to be a "treaty, concluded at New Echota, in the State of Georgia, on the 29th day of December, 1835, by General William Carroll and John F. Schermerhorn, commissioners on the part of the United States, and the chiefs, headmen, and people of the Cherokee tribes of Indians." A spurious Delegation, in violation of a special injunction of the general council of the nation, proceeded to Washington City with this pretended treaty, and by false and fraudulent representations supplanted in the favor of the Government the legal and accredited Delegation of the Cherokee people, and obtained for this instrument, after making important alterations in its provisions, the recognition of the United States Government. And now it is presented to us as a treaty, ratified by the Senate, and approved by the President [Andrew Jackson], and our acquiescence in its requirements demanded, under the sanction of the displeasure of the United States, and the threat of summary compulsion, in case of refusal. It comes to us, not through our legitimate authorities, the known and usual medium of communication between the Government of the United States and our nation, but through the agency of a complication of powers, civil and military.

By the stipulations of this instrument, we are despoiled of our private possessions, the indefeasible property of individuals. We are stripped of every attribute of freedom and eligibility for legal self-defence. Our property may be plundered before our eyes; violence may be committed on our persons; even our lives may be taken away, and there is none to regard our complaints. We are denationalized; we are disfranchised. We are deprived of membership in the human family! We have neither land nor home, nor resting place that can be called our own. And this is effected by the provisions of a compact which assumes the venerated, the sacred appellation of treaty.

We are overwhelmed! Our hearts are sickened, our utterance is paralized, when we reflect on the condition in which we are placed, by the audacious practices of unprincipled men, who have managed their stratagems with so much dexterity as to impose on the Government of the United States, in the face of our earnest, solemn, and reiterated protestations.

The instrument in question is not the act of our Nation; we are not parties to its covenants; it has not received the sanction of our people. The makers of it sustain no office nor appointment in our Nation, under the designation of Chiefs, Head men, or any other title, by which they hold, or could acquire, authority to assume the reins of Government, and to make bargain and sale of our rights, our possessions, and our common country. And we are constrained solemnly to declare, that we cannot but contemplate the enforcement of the stipulations of this instrument on us, against our consent, as an act of injustice and oppression, which, we are well persuaded, can never knowingly be countenanced by the Government and people of the United States; nor can we believe it to be the design of these honorable and highminded individuals, who stand at the head of the Govt., to bind a whole Nation, by the acts of a few unauthorized individuals. And, therefore, we, the parties to be affected by the result, appeal with confidence to the justice, the magnanimity, the compassion, of your honorable bodies, against the enforcement, on us, of the provisions of a compact, in the formation of which we have had no agency.[114]

114 Gary E. Moulton, ed., *The Papers of Chief John Ross, Vol. 1, 1807–1839* (Norman: University of Oklahoma Press, 1985), 458–461. http://historymatters.gmu.edu/d/6598/

General John E. Wool

A letter to the Adjutant-General of the United States

February 18, 1837

I called them (the Cherokees) together and made a short speech. It is, however, vain to talk to a people almost universally opposed to the treaty and who maintain that they never made such a treaty. So determined are they in their opposition that not one of all those who were present and voted at the council held but a day or two since, however poor or destitute, would receive either rations or clothing from the United States, lest they might compromise themselves in regard to the treaty.[115]

115 *Fifth Annual Report of the Bureau of Ethnology, 1883-1884* (Washington: Government Printing Office, 1887), 286.

Anonymous

Decatur, Alabama

A Detachment of 'Treaty Party' members, including the Ridge family, head west

May, 1837

The (Treaty) Party of Cherokees to which we have referred the two past weeks, arrived at this place on Tuesday evening, last in flat boats, towed by the steamer Knoxville from Gunter's landing. It being an excessively wet evening, and quite late when the boats effected a landing, our citizens had not the pleasure of witnessing their arrival. Early on Wednesday morning, however, the Indians, under the direction of Gen. Smith and Doct. John S. Young, the conducting agent of the government, commenced debarking, and by seven o'clock a handsome train of cars were snugly loaded with about half of them and their effects.

To the numerous spectators that thronged either side of the railroad, among whom were to be seen a goodly number of ladies, this aboriginal group presented a truly interesting spectacle. But their appearance, in connection with the locomotive and its train, was not more attractive to the spectators, than did the engine and cars seem to be to the Indians. Many of them could be seen examining, with their peculiar inquisitive silence and gravity, this great enigma to them, while others, apparently uninterested and thoughtless, amused themselves with an old fiddle or sat motionless, gazing at those around. But a lively spirit seemed to animate the balance, with the exception of a few small children, who, though unable to speak a work of our language, as a bystander facetiously observed, 'cried in very good English.'

The remainder of the party left in the afternoon and the next morning. They are to be conveyed by steam-boats, direct from Tuscumbia to Fort Gibson. The whole tribe, according to the late treaty, hope to follow them within two years after its ratification[116]

---

116 *Arkansas State Gazette*, May 9, 1837

George W. Featherstonhaugh

From A Canoe Voyage Up the Minnay Sotor
An account of travel from Brainerd Mission to Red Clay council ground

On reaching (Brainerd) Mission, which had the appearance of a farm-house...an Indian woman called Mr. Buttrick, the resident … Missionary, a pious elderly person apparently out of health, with whom I had a very interesting conversation about his Mission and the situation of the Cherokees… I soon found out that every one at the Mission was zealously disposed in favour of the Indians, and anxious to prevent their being sent out of the country… It was evident that the people at the Mission had transferred all their natural sympathies for their own race to the persecuted Indians. I was not much surprised at it…

...Mr. Buttrick was a decided friend of the Indians, and considered the whites to have violated the most sacred of rights in dispossessing the Cherokee nation of their native country. It had been been found difficult to frame an apology for the conduct of the whites who had, in the earliest times, come amongst the defenceless men and taken their lands, for they had done it under the pretext of converting them to Christianity; but, in the case of the Cherokees, not only treaties had been trampled upon, but every wrong had been heaped upon an unoffending Christian nation. He said he knew the Cherokees well, and thought they would die on the spot rather than leave their country; but, if it came to that, the whites were the strongest and must prevail. "Nevertheless," added he, "God has his eye upon all that is passing, and at his own time the Cherokees will be avenged."

I was very much impressed by his manner, for he evidently was sincere, believing himself in a deep decline, as a bad cough, which frequently troubled him, too truly indicated. I remarked to him that none of the Indian tribes had been able to stand against the tide of the white population, and that perhaps the hand of Providence was in it; for, although the people of Georgia had treated the Indians wrongfully, yet a few generations hence, their descendants might fill the land and be a good and religious people; that the Indians would probably be a much happier community in a distant territory, where they had no white neighbours, and that I was of the opinion that those who had influence with them would render them an essential service by advising them to submit where resistance was hopeless; that to encourage them to resist would be to assist in their extermination, and that I sincerely believed the wisest plan would be to endeavour to persuade them to throw themselves upon the generosity of the United States Government, who had the highest motives to deal in the most merciful and humane way with them. To this he merely observed, that the Council of the Cherokee nation would determine what was to be done...[117]

117 George W. Featherstonhaugh, *A Canoe Voyage up the Minnay Sotor* (St. Paul: Minnesota Historical Society, 1970), 213-215.

Daniel S. Butrick

Missionary

From his journal

Many years ago, the government of the United States, by their agents, advised the Cherokees to scatter from their towns, and make individual improvements for the purpose of raising cattle, horses, hogs, etc. and also in order to cultivate more land in raising grain, cotton, etc. than they could while crowded up in towns.

They also advised them to get looms, spin, weave, make cloth and household furniture, in order to live more comfortably.

They advised them again to improve their government, establish courts of justice, and make laws for the better regulation of their national affairs; and also urged their attention to schools and the education of their children.

The United States, in order to encourage the Indians in improving their condition, and for other reasons, guaranteed their country to them forever, and pledged the faith of the U. States that they should be protected on it, as long as they wished to remain here…

But their rising prosperity soon excited the envy and malice of their white neighbors. They were slandered, and their motives impeached, and they were condemned for following the advice of the highest officer in the U. States…

It was made a capital crime by the legislature of Georgia for the council to convene at the national council house, or for any officer to attempt to execute the laws of the nation…

The desire of the Cherokees to become farmers, in accordance with the advice of the U. States… was deemed stubbornness, and an insufferable affront to those who wanted their land…

Georgia...commenced her grinding oppressive measures, taking for her guide this principle, "Power gives right." They also annulled the laws of the nation, stripped the chiefs of all authority, robbed the nation of civil liberty, and usurped the entire control over it…

These measures were supported by what was called the Georgia guard, a band of soldiers armed for war, and constantly riding through the country…

The Legislature ordered a survey of the country in direct violation of the intercourse law, and treaties with the Cherokees. The land was then disposed by lot, and though the Cherokees were not to be driven away at that time, yet they were limited to their present improvements, and forbid clearing or occupying any new land…

The Cherokees were not allowed to punish, nor attempt to punish any crime whatever. Therefore some most notorious murderers were suffered to pass with impunity…

Gold mines were found on Cherokee land worth millions of Dollars. These were taken by the sovereignty of Georgia, and any Indian found digging gold was condemned to severe punishments.

The Cherokees at length became willing to dispose of some part of their country, but nothing would satisfy the avarice of the white man but the whole. Agents were scattered through the country, to hire, flatter, persuade, or frighten the Cherokees individually to sell their improvements to the whites and go to the west.[118]

118 Daniel S. Butrick, *The Journal of Rev. Daniel S. Butrick, May 19, 1838 – April 1, 1839* (Park Hill: The Trail of Tears Association, Oklahoma Chapter, 1998), 13-17.

John Ross & Others

Chief of the Cherokee Nation

From a Memorial presented to US. Congress

Wahka and his wife were natives of, and residents in, the Cherokee nation east of the Mississippi. The agents of the United States prevailed upon the wife to enrol for emigration, against the remonstrances of the husband, and they afterwards, by force, separated her from her husband, and took her arid the children to Arkansas, leaving the husband and father behind, because he would not enrol. The improvements upon which he resided were valued in the name of the wife, and he turned out of possession.

Atalah Anosta was prevailed upon to enrol when drunk, contrary to the wish and will of his wife and children; when the time arrived for him to leave for Arkansas, he absconded. A guard was sent after him by B. F. Currey, which arrested the woman and children, and brought them to the agency about dark, in a cold rain, shivering and hungry. They were detained under guard all night, and part of the next day, and until the woman agreed to enrol her name as an emigrant. The husband then came in, and he and his wife and their children were put on board a boat and taken to Arkansas. There they soon lost two or three of their children, and then returned on foot to the Cherokee nation east of the Mississippi.

Sconatachee, when drunk, was enrolled by Benjamin F. Currey; when the emigrants were collecting, he did not appear, and Currey and John Miller, the interpreter, went after him. Currey drew a pistol and attempted to drive the old man to the agency, who presented his gun and refused to go. Currey and Miller returned without him. He made the facts known to Hugh Montgomery, the Cherokee agent, who gave him a certificate that he should not be forced away against his will. So the matter rested till the emigrants were collected the next year, and then Currey sent a wagon and guard for him. He was arrested, tied, and hauled to the agency, leaving some of his children behind in the woods, where they had fled on the approach of the guard.

Richard Cheek enrolled for emigration, but before the time of departure, he hired to work on the Tuscumbia rail-road, in Alabama. When the emigrants started, Currey had Cheek's wife taken, put on board a boat, and started to Arkansas. She was even denied the privilege of visiting her husband as she descended the river. He was left behind, and never saw her more. She died on the way.

Such outrages, and violations of treaty stipulations, have been the subject of complaint to the Government of the United States, on the part of the Cherokees. for years past; and the delegation are not surprised, that the American people are not now startled at those wrongs, so long continued, for by habit men are brought to look with indifference upon death itself. If the Government of the United States have determined to take the Cherokee lands without their consent, the power is with them; and the American people can "reap the field that is not their own, and gather the vintage of his vineyard whom by violence they have oppressed."[119]

---

119 *Memorial Protest of the Cherokee Nation, 1836.* United States Congressional Serial Set, House Document 286, 24th Congress, 1st session.

George W. Featherstonhaugh

From A Canoe Voyage Up the Minnay Sotor

An account of travel from Brainerd Mission to Red Clay council ground

We met many parties of Cherokees of the lowest class going on foot to the great meeting. Some of them were very drunk and were accompanied by young women carrying their infants. Log huts now increased in number with clearings around them, surrounded by broken-down fences, and bearing evidence of slovenly farming. The white inhabitants were a tall, sallow, gawky-looking set, with manners of the coarsest kind; their children were all pale and unhealthy-looking, suffering, as the mothers told me, from bowel complaints, occasioned evidently by unwholesome food and filth. We passed several farms belonging to the principal Cherokees, containing fine patches of the sweet potato… maize and pulse of various kinds. Some of the Indians women spoke English, but generally they were shy, and in a few instances refused to answer me. I was not surprised at this…

On my return to the village, I observed that almost every store in the place was a dram shop, and the evening's amusement of a great part of the population seemed to consist in going about from one to the other; and when they got what they call in this part of the country "high," which means red-hot drunk with whisky, they would go to the tavern and bully the people they found there…

A young white fellow came to the tavern with a frightful wound in his leg, and so drunk that all we could get from him, amidst a torrent of the most audacious blasphemies, was that "his horse had fixed it for him." ... The (white) people about were tall, thin, cadaverous-looking animals, looking as melancholy and lazy as boiled cod-fish, and when they dragged themselves about, formed a striking contrast to some of the swarthy, athletic-looking Cherokees. This, no doubt, is to be attributed to their wretched diet and manner of life… What these long parsnip-looking country fellows seem to enjoy most is political disputation in the bar-room of their filthy taverns...Execration and vociferation, and "Well, I'm for Jackson, by (God)!" were the nearest approach to logic ever made in my presence. Their miserable attempts at farming… are as absurd as they are ridiculous…

…(A) company of Georgia Mounted Volunteers rode through the place on their way to the Cherokee Council. All had their coats off with their muskets and cartouch-boxes strung across their shoulders. Some of the men had straw hats, some of them white felt hats, others had old black hats on with the rim torn off, and all of them were as unshaven and dirty as they could well be… Many of the men were young fellows, and they rode on, talking, and cursing and swearing, without any kind of discipline…

...Crossing the Cooayhallay, we soon found ourselves in an irregular sort of street consisting of huts, booths and stores hastily constructed from the trees of the forest, for the accommodation of Cherokee families, and for the cooking establishments necessary to the subsistence of several thousand Indians. This street was at the foot of some hilly ground upon which the Council-room was built, which was a simple parallelogram formed of logs with open sides, and benches inside for the councillors. The situation was exceedingly well chosen in every respect, for there was a copious limestone spring on the bank of the stream, which gave out a delicious cool water in sufficient quantities for this great multitude. What contributed to make the situation extremely picturesque, was the great number of beautiful trees growing in every direction, the underwood having been most judiciously cut away to enable the Indians to move freely through the forest, and to tie their horses to the trees. Nothing more Arcadian could be conceived than the picture which was presented; but the most impressive feature, and that which imparted life to the whole, was an unceasing current of Cherokee Indians, men, women, youths, and children, moving about in every direction, and in the greatest order; and all, except the younger ones, preserving a grave and thoughtful demeanor imposed upon them by the singular position in which they were placed, and by the trying alternative now presented to them of delivering up their native country to their oppressors, or perishing in a vain resistance.

An observer could not help but sympathize deeply with them; they were not to be confounded with the wild savages of the West, being decently dressed after the manner of white people, with shirts, trousers, shoes and stockings, whilst the half-breeds and their descendants conformed in every thing to the custom of the whites, spoke as good English as them, and differed from them only in a browner complexion, and in being less vicious and more sober. The pure bloods had red and blue cotton handkerchiefs folded on their heads in the manner of turbans, and some of these, who were mountaineers from the elevated districts of North Carolina, wore also deer-skin leggings and embroidered hunting shirts; whilst their turbans, their dark coarse, lank hair, their listless savage gait, and their swarthy Tartar countenances, reminded me of the Arabs from the Barbary. Many of these men were athletic and good-looking…

The voices of the Cherokees already at morning worship awoke me at the dawn of the (following) day, and dressing myself hastily, I went to the Council-house. Great numbers of them were assembled, and Mr. Jones, the missionary, read out verses in the English language from the New Testament, which Bushy-head, with a singularly stentorial voice and sonorous accent, immediately rendered to the people in the Cherokee tongue… When they sang, a line or two of a hymn printed in the Cherokee language was given out, each one having a hymn book in his hand, and I certainly never saw any congregation engaged more apparently in sincere devotion. This spectacle insensibly led me into reflection upon the opinion which is so generally entertained of its being impossible to civilize the Indians in our sense of the word. Here is a remarkable instance which seems to furnish a conclusive answer to scepticism on this point. A whole Indian nation abandons the pagan practices of their ancestors, adopts the Christian religion, uses books printed in their own language, submits to the government of their elders, builds houses and temples of worship, relies upon agriculture for their support, and produces men of great ability to rule over them, and to whom they give a willing obedience. Are not these the great principles of civilization? They are driven from their religious and social state then, not because they cannot be civilized, but because a pseudo set of civilized beings, who are too strong for them, want their possessions! What a bitter reflection it will be to the religiously disposed portion of the people who shall hereafter live here, that the country they will be so proud of and so blest in was torn from the Aboriginals in this wrongful manner.[120]

---

120 George W. Featherstonhaugh, *A Canoe Voyage up the Minnay Sotor* (St. Paul: Minnesota Historical Society, 1970), 222-234.

Barney Hughes

Cherokee Nation citizen
Will's Valley
1837

I left the plantation on Terrapins Creek (Alabama) on account of an armed company of men from the States, who came in that part of the country in a hostile manner killing and imprisoning my people. That for fear of my own safety I left and settled in Will's Valley…

I was residing on Will's Creek in the Cherokees east in the year 1837 in the midst of many white persons who had entered on the Cherokee lands. There was a store kept in the place by a white man. This store was broken (into), and a considerable amount of goods taken by Cherokees, as I was informed. I was then together with my son John Hughes taken by a company of whitemen of the place and after holding a consultation on the case, they determined to whip me and my son, which they executed by stripping both of us, and whipping us with sticks and switches on the bare back until we were cruelly punished. We were still kept in duress until the next day and then allowed to go to our house.[121]

---

121 Marybelle W. Chase, *1842 Cherokee Claims, Saline District* (from originals located at the Tennessee State Library and Archives, Nashville, Tennessee), 157-158.

Harry Hughes

Cherokee Nation citizen

Will's Valley

1837

Many white people had settled (near the place) in which Barney Hughes and son resided. These white persons formed a company and arrested Barney Hughes and John Hughes, men of good character, who they fettered with strings, stripped them of their clothing, and then with sticks and switches whipped both with great severity.[122]

122 Ibid.

Order No. 15

October 5, 1837

Capt. Buffington with his company Geo. Vols. will, without any unnecessary delay repair to the neighborhood of Canton, Cherokee County, Geo. and select a suitable position for a cantonment. He will proceed to erect huts and stables for his company and other buildings necessary for the post, as soon as practicable, according to a plan herewith furnished.[123]

---

123 Sarah H. Hill, *Cherokee Removal from Georgia*, 2005. (Original record at National Archives RG 92 Entry 357 Box 6). https://www.nps.gov/trte/learn/historyculture/upload/Georgia-Forts.pdf

From the Editor

The Federal Union

January 30, 1838

The Cherokees: we understand that every prospect of the unwillingness to remove without force seems to exist. It is thought that Ross will not do otherwise than remain silent on the subject of their going, and that it is his policy to permit them to be driven to the very last extremity - even to the point of the bayonet, and to be carried by force from the country. We understand that their deportment towards the whites is much more reserved than usual and when addressed in relation to their removal to the West, they decline all conversation on the subject. Rumor, indeed, says that in the Nation, beyond the Georgia line, preparations appear to be making by them for hostilities, and in many parts the inhabitants are much alarmed for their safety; in our Cherokee counties so much so that numbers are now removing their families to the interior for better security against the danger now apprehended from these Indians.

We trust this sense of danger and the reports of their hostile movements are not well founded in fact. Until the time arrives for them to leave we are inclined to think there will exist no cause of dread or danger from them, unless murders and other depredations are committed in consequence of the imprudent course which our citizens may pursue , either by exhibiting alarm by removing from the country or by provoking hostilities. We hope that our Cherokee citizens will be on their guard as to the movements of these savages; and we anxiously trust the people will remain in the country, prepared to defend themselves and their homes when the times comes in which danger may be expected, and their assistance be required in quelling them. We publish in today's paper the order of the Executive, again inviting volunteers to enter the service for the defense of the Cherokee country. From the active and energetic measures which appear to be taken for placing the country in a state of preparation for defence against the hostilities of the Indians, every portion of the nation will be well fortified with a sufficient force to expel them and strike terror to their feelings of animosity towards our citizens before the first of

May, the time when, if at all, it is believed they will be likely to commit acts of violence against the property and persons of our citizens.[124]

---

124 *The Federal Union*, Jan. 30, 1838.

Tesaweskee

As related by Belle Kendrick Abbott

Tesaweskee was the name of an Indian who died in the Canton jail February, 1838 as he was being carried from Cassville to the penitentiary in Milledgeville. It was alleged and proven that he died from cruel treatment at hands of the two men who had him in charge, as the record states among other sickening details, 'that when the chain was taken from his neck the flesh was beaten to a jelly.' The record was a sad one. It did not state what the Indian has done, only said he was a convict being sent from Cassville to the penitentiary in the care of two men. These men were finally acquitted. This record in the case of poor Tesaweskee shows how poor a chance for justice and mercy the red man has ever had, at the hands of a race who consider themselves of higher mould and better blood.[125]

125 *The Atlanta Constitution*, Nov. 17, 1889.

Anonymous

March 13, 1838

Indian Anecdote: A son of the Emerald Isle, traveling in the Cherokee country, met a native, "Good morning'" said the traveller. "O-see-u" replied the Indian (meaning Good morning). "You see me," replied the Irishman, "I see you too." "Skene-unake" (meaning White man), said the Indian, somewhat offended by the rough language of his fellow traveller. "Skin my neck," cried the Irishman in a burst of passion. "By the height of the hill of Houth I'll skin your neck first." and he forthwith began to pummel the unfortunate native most unmercifully. "Nok wa" (meaning Quit), yelled the Indian. "Yes," said the Irishman, "damn your eyes, I'll knock you 'til your heart's contented with the bating. I'll give ye ____."[126]

126 *The Federal Union*, March 13, 1838.

From the Editor

The Federal Union

April 24, 1838

We've heard that Ross will remove his people, which could be done quickly. This would be good since we would not have to hunt them down like wild deer and wolves, which would be costly. [127]

127 *The Federal Union,* April 24, 1838.

Samuel Tate

From a letter to Georgia Gov. George Gilmer

February 11, 1838

I assure you . . . the Indians could ruin the whole country if they were to try. There should be one company stationed at Coosawatter that is the strongest Indian settlement in this country and some of them are very savage. Another betwixt Canton and Ellijay and another betwixt Ellijay and Valley River. It is the mountain Indians that will do mischief. . . . If it is in your power to send troops here I think it would be advisable.[128]

128 Grace Steele Woodward, *The Cherokees* (Norman: University of Oklahoma Press), 99-100.

'...until we are forced to do so.'

William Jasper Cotter

White resident of Rock Spring,

near Coosawattee

A Remembrance of Spring, 1838

The spring of 1838 opened most beautifully. There was no cold weather after the first of March. Vegetation advanced without any backsets from the cold. The buds burst into leaves and blossoms; the woods were green and gay and merry with the singing birds. The Indians started to work in their fields earlier than ever before. Usually they were lazy and late in starting with their crops, working around logs in their fields and letting bushes and briers grow in the fence corners. That spring you could see the smoke of their log heaps or piles of ashes where the boys had been. Fence corners and hedgerows were cleaned out. The ground was well plowed and the corn planted better than ever before. Soon it was knee-high and growing nicely. [129]

129 William Jasper Cotter, *My Autobiography* (Nashville: Publishing House Methodist Episcopal Church, South, 1917), 38-39. https://archive.org/details/myautobiographyccoocott

Lt. Edward Deas

U.S. Army

Conductor of a Cherokee party

Waterloo, Alabama

April 6, 1838

Yesterday a Party of Cherokee Indians, in number Two hundred & fifty, together with some other emigrants of the same tribe who are removing on their own resources, arrived near Waterloo, Ala. by water, under charge of the Superintendent of the Cherokee Emigration. The S. Boat *Smelter*, provided under the contract for Transportation, had been waiting the arrival of the Party, and to day the Indians were established on board of this boat, and one large Keel with double cabins, made & furnished in the manner mentioned in the above named contract.

The Present Party, having been previously Enrolled, were to-day turned over to me as Conductor, and immediately afterwards (about 10 O'Clock A.M.) the boat was got under weigh and continued to run until after sunset, having come more than 100 miles and laid by on account of the darkening of the night...[130]

---

130 Journal of Occurrences of Lt. Edward Deas, April 1838, Special Case Files of The Office of Indian Affairs, 1807-1994, Roll 69, National Archives Microfilm Publications D217 http://ualrexhibits.org/trailoftears/eyewitness-accounts/journal-of-edward-deas-cherokee-removal-april-may-1838/

Lt. Edward Deas

US. Army

Conductor of a Cherokee party

Titsworth's at McLean's Bottom, Arkansas

April 20, 1838

...I determined to land the Party at this place for the reason, that there would be but little probability of the Steam Boat getting the whole distance to the Cherokee Country, and as the end of the journey would therefore have to be performed by land, under any arrangement, it is better to stop at a point where wagons can be procured...

When we landed at McLean's Bottom, I found the people unprovided with Tents, or any protection from the weather, and as the Physician was of the opinion that their health would suffer from exposure, I considered it my duty to purchase for their use, as much cotton domestic as was sufficient to shelter them from the rain.[131]

131 Ibid.

Statement of Forage

A military inventory of
forage available in the Cherokee Nation
at a camp near LaFayette, Georgia

Camp Near LaFayette: 200 bushels corn, no bundles fodder; 3000 bushels corn the probable amount to be obtained in the vicinity, 10000 bundles fodder the probable amount to be obtained in the vicinity; 1.12 ½ the probable cost of corn, 3.00 the probable cost of fodder, 12 the probable number of teams.[132]

132 Sarah H. Hill, *Cherokee Removal from Georgia*, 2005. (Original record at National Archives Records Administration RG 393 m1475 r1 p. 137). https://www.nps.gov/trte/learn/historyculture/upload/Georgia-Forts.pdf

Capt. John S. Means

Georgia Volunteers

Letter to Col. William Lindsay

Fort Means, on the Floyd / Cass County Line

May 22, 1838

In pursuance of your order the following report will show so far as I have been able to ascertain the number and disposition of the Indians within the bounds which have been assigned me.

On Mr. Putnam's plantation ½ mile south of this place on the west side of Hightower or Utiwah River 5 Cabbins ____ No. of Ind 50 Indians

At Mr. Williams 2 ½ miles south ...: 4 cabbins, 30 indians.

Mr. Mann's 3 ½ m same side R. South – 2 cabbins – 12.

Mr. Lumpkin's on the E. side R. 5 miles s. 9 cabins.

Mr. Price plantation 3 miles E. side river 3 cabbins 25.

Mr. Tarpin's ditto. 4 cabins 2 miles east side Utiwah river. 30.

General Millers place 1 mile E. side of river 9 cabbins 90.

Major Woody's place – 9 cabins 4 miles east of east side of river, Utiwah or Hightower. 90 Indians.

Judgs. Underwoods E. side river Utiwah or Hightower 8 cabbins 75 Indians.

Geo. Underwood a mile E and E. side Utiwah or Hightower River 2 cabbins. 10 Indians

W. Burges – 10 miles east of Utiwah or Hightower E side 1 cabbin ...

Conicena 4 miles E and W side Utiwah River No Indians

Hightower River 2 cabbins no Indians 15

J. Miller's 1 m NE 2 cabbins 6.

Col. Waters plantation on Oostanaula River 8 miles NW 2 cabbins. 15.

Lavinders 10 m NW 2 cabbins 15

Col. Hardin's 9 miles 5 cabbins 30.

The above is as near the number of Indians as I could ascertain without an interpreter which I could not obtain from the best information that I can get from them and from the citizens who are acquainted with them and four-fifths of them are averse from emigating until they hear from their Chief Ross and not even then until they are dispossessed. I think this is with a view of claiming further damage. This I have had from one who speaks English. Yet I cannot believe from anything which I have discovered in any of them that they will offer any hostility. Some outlawed fellows may be disposed to do private injury but I think I shall have it in my power to put it so far down as that. Instances of the kind will (not occur) if the citizens should not act imprudently and attempt forcing them from their farms before it is done by the order of the commanding officer. However I have took all the pains that I could do to advise against... I have finished my fort all to hanging the gate which I am now about doing with the exception of the block house I have commenced doing this and can soon complete it if the infantry company could I shall use all industry until they arrive ...

As ordered I report to you and shall take pleasure in attending to all orders from you or any other commanding officer.[133]

133 From a copy obtained from Sarah H. Hill, quoted in part in her *Cherokee Removal from Georgia*, 2005; original at National Archives Records Administration RG 393 m1475 r1 fr0319-22. https://www.nps.gov/trte/learn/historyculture/upload/Georgia-Forts.pdf

Capt. H. B. Henegar

Recollections of Cherokee Removal

Related October 25, 1897

Charleston, Bradley County, Tennessee, on the Hiwassee River, was the starting-point and the place where the Ross party was collected. General Scott was stationed here with the United States Troops. The spot where my residence now stands was the barracks. The regular soldiers were assisted by several companies of militia; but not much difficulty was encountered in collecting the Indians...[134]

---

134 Capt. H.B. Henegar, "Recollections of the Cherokee Removal." *Journal of Cherokee Studies* 3, no. 3 (1978): 47.

Major General Winfield Scott

May 10, 1838

An Address to the Cherokees

Cherokees! The President of the United States has sent me with a powerful army, to cause you, in obedience to the treaty of 1835 [the Treaty of New Echota], to join that part of your people who have already established in prosperity on the other side of the Mississippi. Unhappily, the two years which were allowed for the purpose, you have suffered to pass away without following, and without making any preparation to follow; and now, or by the time that this solemn address shall reach your distant settlements, the emigration must be commenced in haste, but I hope without disorder. I have no power, by granting a farther delay, to correct the error that you have committed. The full moon of May is already on the wane; and before another shall have passed away, every Cherokee man, woman and child in those states must be in motion to join their brethren in the far West.

My friends! This is no sudden determination on the part of the President, whom you and I must now obey. By the treaty, the emigration was to have been completed on or before the 23rd of this month; and the President has constantly kept you warned, during the two years allowed, through all his officers and agents in this country, that the treaty would be enforced.

I am come to carry out that determination. My troops already occupy many positions in the country that you are to abandon, and thousands and thousands are approaching from every quarter, to render resistance and escape alike hopeless. All those troops, regular and militia, are your friends. Receive them and confide in them as such. Obey them when they tell you that your can remain no longer in this country. Soldiers are as kind-hearted as brave, and the desire of every one of us is to execute our painful duty in mercy. We are commanded by the President to act towards you in that spirit, and much is also the wish of the whole people of America.

Chiefs, head-men and warriors! Will you then, by resistance, compel us to resort to arms? God forbid! Or will you, by flight, seek to hide yourselves in mountains and forests, and thus oblige us to hunt you down? Remember that, in pursuit, it may be impossible to avoid conflicts. The blood of the white man or the blood of the red man may be spilt, and, if spilt, however accidentally, it may be impossible for the discreet and humane among you, or among us, to prevent a general war and carnage. Think of this, my Cherokee brethren! I am an old warrior, and have been present at many a scene of slaughter, but spare me, I beseech you, the horror of witnessing the destruction of the Cherokees.

Do not, I invite you, even wait for the close approach of the troops; but make such preparations for emigration as you can and hasten to this place, to Ross's Landing or to Gunter's Landing, where you all will be received in kindness by officers selected for the purpose. You will find food for all and clothing for the destitute at either of those places, and thence at your ease and in comfort be transported to your new homes, according to the terms of the treaty.

This is the address of a warrior to warriors. May his entreaties be kindly received and may the God of both prosper the Americans and Cherokees and preserve them long in peace and friendship with each other![135]

---

135 Major General Winfield Scott, "Address to the Cherokees." *Journal of Cherokee Studies* 3, no. 3 (1978): 15. http://ualrexhibits.org/trailoftears/indian-removal/cherokee-removal-chronicle-1830-1839/

Orders No. 34

From Major General Scott

New Echota

Headquarters, Eastern Division

May 24, 1838

A sufficient number of troops having arrived or known to be approaching the collection of the Indians within the Cherokee Country, preparatory to their emigration beyond the Mississippi, will be commenced in Georgia on the 26th Inst. or as soon thereafter as this order may be received, & in the adjoining states, ten days later.

The commanding officer at every fort & open station will first cause to be surrounded and brought in as many Indians, the nearest to his fort or station, as he may think he can secure at once, & repeat the operation until he shall have made as many prisoners as he is able to subsist and send off, under a proper escort, to the most convenient of the emigrating depots, the Cherokee Agency, Ross Landing, and Gunters Landing.

These operations will be again and again repeated under the order of the commanders of the respective districts, until the whole of the Indians shall have been collected for emigration.

In many cases it may be almost impracticable for the commander of an open station to escort his prisoners to one of the distant emigrating depots mentioned above. It is permitted therefore to such commander, when necessary, to send his prisoners under a proper escort to the nearest fort in the direction of one of those depots, there to wait for a further escort.

On the arrival of the Indian prisoners, at an emigrating depot, they will be received in the first instance by the commanding officer of the place.

In every case when detachments are sent out to bring in Indians, a sufficient guard will be retained to hold the fort or to guard the subsistence & all the property left at the open station.

Every commander of a fort or open station will report his operations & whatever else of interest that may occur around him to the commander of his District, & the latter will frequently make reports to the Major General...[136]

136 Orders No. 34, *Journal of Cherokee Studies* 3, no. 3 (1978): 17-18.

Daniel S. Butrick

Missionary

Brainerd Mission, Tennessee

May 26, 1838

This day a number of Georgia citizens near New Echota took sixteen Cherokees and drove them to the fort and then requested permission of General Scott to take them out and whip them, though in this they were not gratified. This was done probably to remind General Scott that no further delay would be made with regard to collecting the Indians.[137]

---

137 Daniel S. Butrick, *The Journal of Rev. Daniel S. Butrick, May 19, 1838 – April 1, 1839* (Park Hill: The Trail of Tears Association, Oklahoma Chapter, 1998), 1.

N. W. Pittman

Madison's Company

June 6, 1838

When we arrived we learned that an express had arrived ordering operations to commence against the Indians. We prepared something to eat with the greatest possible dispatch after which three companies of our Battalion were detailed to go in pursuit and taking Indian prisoners...[138]

---

138 Letter to Henchin Strickland of Danielsville, Madison County, Ga., from his son-in-law, N.W. Pittman, and son H.P. Strickland, Series 1. Papers, 1838-1954, in the John R. Peacock papers #1895-z, Southern Historical Collection, The Wilson Library, University of North Carolina at Chapel Hill. http://finding-aids.lib.unc.edu/01895/

Lt. John Phelps

US. 4th Artillery

Near Fort Hembree, North Carolina

May 28, 1838

We passed to day several indifferent log huts with no other opening than a single doorway to each. At one of them there appeared nine women and two men, all having pale faces and grey eyes. They appeared to me to be very lazy, laboring only to procure a sufficience which these vallies will very readily yield. Such brutality as every thing on the route to day indicated, I never saw before among white people unless they were Irishmen.[139]

139 Sarah H. Hill, ed., "The Diary of Lt. John Phelps." *The Journal of Cherokee Studies 21*, Special Issue (2000): 14.

Lt. John Phelps

US. 4th Artillery

Fort Hembree, North Carolina

May 29, 1838

Passed several Cherokees. They were neatly dressed in our costume and looked very respectable. The white inhabitants whom I have asked concerning them, give them good characters as neighbors. It is said they affect to believe that the troops are sent here by Ross in order to protect them against speculators.

We passed Fort Hembree and encamped about five o'clock on Hiawassee River near fort Butler. The mountain on the right bank of the stream just opposite us consists chiefly of rock…

The nights are uncomfortably cold.[140]

140 Ibid., 15

A. E. Blunt

Missionary,

American Board of Commissioners for Foreign Missions

Candy's Creek Mission Station, Tennessee

May 23, 1838

The long looked for day (23rd of May) however as much was it desired by some and feared by others has arrived.

Notwithstanding the prospects before us have looked appalling, it has been a matter of surprise to see the steady onward course of the Cherokees. I have heard it remembered by persons traveling in various parts of the Nation (Ga. excepted) that the people were never so forward in their crops and never appeared as industrious as at the present crisis. The movements in the whole country for several weeks past seemed to indicate war. The arrival of the military — cannon, powder, lead, and boxes of arms — has indeed looked like the shedding of blood. But… no enemy has been found to contend with, and while some of the volunteers have been most insulting, in some instances, the people have borne it patiently and have gone on, attending to their business.

For some days previous to the 23rd, the military were riding through the country ordering the Cherokees to report to certain points for emigration before the expiration of the time specified before the fraudulent treaty. All seems to have no effect. Onward, seems to be the motto of all the Cherokees. We have justice on our side let come what will, and some have told the officers that they should continue to attend to their own business until forced at the point of the bayonet.

During all the storms which has clouded the nation there has been no sudden alarms or fright with the Cherokees, while on the other hand the whites in some instances have removed out of the Nation and many have been ready to start at the rustling of a leaf.[141]

---

141 Duane King, *The Cherokee Trail of Tears* (Portland: Graphic Arts Books, 2007), 43. (Original letter in the ABCFM papers, Houghton Library, Cambridge, Massachusetts.)

William Jasper Cotter

White resident of Rock Spring,

near Coosawattee

A Remembrance

After all the warning and with the soldiers in their midst, the inevitable day appointed found the Indians at work in their houses and in their fields.[142]

142 William Jasper Cotter, *My Autobiography* (Nashville: Publishing House Methodist Episcopal Church, South, 1917), 39 https://archive.org/details/myautobiographycc00cott

Daniel S. Butrick

Missionary

Brainerd Mission, Tennessee

Saturday, May 26, 1838

The soldiers at the various posts now commenced that work which will doubtless long eclipse the glory of the United States. General Scott gave orders that no improper language should be used towards the Indians, and that in case any of them attempted to escape by flight, no gun should be discharged at them. But these orders were, in general obeyed or not, according to the disposition of the under officers, and soldiers.[143]

---

143 Daniel S. Butrick, *The Journal of Rev. Daniel S. Butrick, May 19, 1838 – April 1, 1839* (Park Hill: The Trail of Tears Association, Oklahoma Chapter, 1998), 1.

Evan Jones

Baptist missionary to the Cherokees

The work of war in time of peace was commenced in the Georgia part of the nation and was executed in most cases in unfeeling and brutal manner, no regard being paid to the orders of the Commanding General in regard to humane treatment of the Indians and abstaining from insulting conduct. In that state, in many cases, the Indians were not allowed to gather up their clothes, not even to take away a little money they might have. [144]

144 William G. McLoughlin, *Champions of the Cherokees: Evan and John B. Jones* (Princeton: Princeton University Press, 1990), 176.

Daniel S. Butrick

Missionary,

Brainerd Mission, Tennessee

May 26, 1838

In Georgia were supposed to be about 8,000 Cherokees. Those, in general, were taken just as they were found by the soldiers, without permission to stop either for friends or property.[145]

---

145 Daniel S. Butrick, *The Journal of Rev. Daniel S. Butrick, May 19, 1838 – April 1, 1839* (Park Hill: The Trail of Tears Association, Oklahoma Chapter, 1998), 1.

William Jasper Cotter

White resident of Rock Spring,

near Coosawattee

A Remembrance

It is remembered as well as if it had been seen yesterday, that two or three dropped their hoes and ran as fast as they could when they saw the soldiers coming into the field. After that they made no effort to get out of the way. The men handled them gently, but picked them up in the road, in the field, anywhere they found them, part of a family at a time, and carried them to the post.[146]

146 William Jasper Cotter, *My Autobiography* (Nashville: Publishing House Methodist Episcopal Church, South, 1917), 39 https://archive.org/details/myautobiographycc00cott

Anny Stealer

Cherokee Nation citizen

Georgia

...in the month of May, 1838, while peaceably engaged at my domestic affairs at my residence in the Eastern Nation, I was rudely accosted by a white man, citizen of the United States, who struck me several times in the head with a gun, until he knocked me down, and when I was making an attempt to rise, he stabbed me in the thigh with a bayonet...[147]

147 Marybelle W. Chase, *1842 Cherokee Claims, Tahlequah District,* Claim No. 276 (from originals located at the Tennessee State Library and Archives, Nashville, Tennessee), 140.

Oo-loo-cha Sweet Water

Cherokee Nation citizen

Oostanallee, Georgia

I am a full blood Cherokee...and emigrated about the year 1838 — under General Smith. I was then the wife of "Sweet Water" who came to this country with me, and has since died. The soldiers came and took us from home. They first surround our house and they took the mare while they were at work in the field and then drove us out of doors and did not permit us to take any thing with us, not even a second change of clothes, only the clothes we had on, and they shut the doors after they turned us out. They would not permit any of us to enter the house to get any clothing but drove us off to a fort that was built at New Echota. They kept us there in the fort about three days and then marched us to Ross's Landing, and still on foot, even our little children, and they kept us about three days at Ross's Landing, and sent us off on a boat to this country...The cattle and hogs were all running there on the place where we were taken off, and every thing we possessed was all left... We heard of the orders being issued to take us and also heard of the building of the Forts, and some white people would tell us we would all be taken, but we did not believe that it would take place. We were so much opposed to coming to this country. [148]

148 Marybelle W. Chase, *1842 Cherokee Claims, Skin Bayou District* (from originals located at the Tennessee State Library and Archives, Nashville, Tennessee), 210-211.

Oo-wah Otter

Cherokee Nation citizen

Georgia

I was taken by the U.S. troops from my house and forced off by them to a place called New Echota, and was kept there two or three days, and after that time they took me to a place called Ross' Landing and they kept us there two nights and then they forced us on aboard of a boat and started us for this country. I was compelled to leave every thing and was not allowed any time to sell and of (my) things… When the troops came to take me I was in my field ploughing my corn. When the troops took me I had to leave all so I could not take any with me. The gun was taken out of my house by the troops, as they had taken all the guns from the Cherokees that were living near me. When the troops came to my house I was not even allowed to go in to my house so I had to leave all as it was in the place. The troops would not allow me to take any of the … things with me, so it was a total loss to me.[149]

149 Marybelle W. Chase, *1842 Cherokee Claims, Skin Bayou District* (from originals located at the Tennessee State Library and Archives, Nashville, Tennessee), 179

Rebecca Neugin

Recorded by Grant Foreman in 1932

When the soldier came to our house my father wanted to fight, but my mother told him that the soldiers would kill him if he did and we surrendered without a fight. They drove us out of our house to join other prisoners in a stockade. After they took us away, my mother begged them to let her go back and get some bedding, So they let her go back and she brought what bedding and a few cooking utensils she could carry and had to leave behind all our other household possessions.[150]

150 Rebecca Neugin, "Memories of the Trail." *Journal of Cherokee Studies* 3, no. 3 (1978): 46.

Daniel S. Butrick

Missionary,

Brainerd Mission, Tennessee

Saturday, May 26, 1838

The daily words in the United Brethren textbook were, "I am thine. Save me." (p.s. 119:9)[151]

151 Daniel S. Butrick, *The Journal of Rev. Daniel S. Butrick, May 19, 1838 – April 1, 1839* (Park Hill: The Trail of Tears Association, Oklahoma Chapter, 1998), 1.

Walesca

Cherokee Nation citizen

Cherokee County, Georgia

(as related by Lewis Reinhardt to Belle Kendrick Abbott)

Walesca was the name of an Indian who lived in now Cherokee county, and was quite a noted man among his settlement. He was distinguished for always wearing feathers from eagles that he shot himself. He had six children, and among them quite a handsome daughter. Mr. Rheinhardt was one of the earliest settlers in that county, and lived near Walesca, the Indian. He was very kind in his treatment and dealings with the Indians, and they loved and respected him. In his intercourse with them he tried to teach them of God and what was displeasing in His sight. Among the various wicked things which he taught them to look upon with abhorrence was to work on the Sabbath. It so chanced, however, that one Sunday morning Mr. Reinhardt went down to his new ground to look after the burning log heap. In one heap he found that the chunks needed pushing up closer together, and so he got over the fence to do this. As he was in the act a group of Indians came along and caught him thus mending the fire. Instantly they began to upbraid him, shaking their heads dubiously, and they said to him they did not care much for the religion of a man who would work on Sunday in the new ground, but did not want them to do it. To his dying day Mr. Rheinhardt said he never forgot the rebuke, and ever after profited by it. He has many transactions with them, found them docile, kind, grateful, if well-treated, over revengeful when wronged.

When the time of removal came, the Indians around what is now Walesca opposed going away. Some of them stoutly refused, and ran into the woods. It so happened that Mr. Rheinhardt was absent from home that day. The enrolling officer called upon Mrs. Rheinhardt to speak to some of the men, and urge them to obey the law. She did so. A man named Fourkiller, who had declared he would die before he would be captured, and who had sent his family into the woods, at last yielded. He took Mrs. Rheinhardt to one side and gave her the keys to his cabins, and told her where his family and the other fugitives were concealed. If she would go to a certain spot and whistle with her fist in a certain way they would all come up. When Mr. Rheinhardt came back these instructions were obeyed and all the hidden-out Indians came to light. He explained the situation to them and promised to accompany them to Fort Buffington and see that no harm was done them. This promise satisfied them, and soon a crowd of them, headed by Mr. Rheinhardt, struck out for the fort. They could not walk the road, but went by trails through the woods.

As they neared the fort suddenly they all halted and held an excited consultation and refused to go further. By persuasion they soon made known to Mr. Rheinhardt that they had heard the drum beating in the fort, and were afraid. Mr. Rheinhardt assured them, but before moving a step, they began to unpack the bundle of stuff they had with them, from which they took about two pounds of gunpowder and gave it to Mr. Rheinhardt to keep, saying they were afraid to take it into the fort themselves. Then reassured they went on into the fort. Fourkiller asked for four days of grace, in which to dispose of his things as he chose, and obtained it by Mr. Rheinhardt standing as his security for his appearance....

When old, the Cherokee Walesca went off. He left his name behind him in the settlement where he lived.[152]

152 *The Atlanta Constitution*, Nov. 24, 1889.

Genahsee

Cherokee Nation citizen

For 1 Cow $12 20 head stock hogs @ $2 52.

" Bed furniture $10. 2 Pots @ $2 14

" 1 Brass kettle $5 crockery $2 7.

" 14 cups @ 12 1/2 cts. 2 Pails @ 75¢ 3.25

" 1 Keeler 50¢ 10 chickens @ 12 1/2¢ 1.75

" 1 loom & wheel & pr. cards 14.

" 1 axe $2 4 (fanners?) @ 25¢ 3.00 95.

The claimant in this case states (on oath) that she lived at Ahmuchee and came to this country in Bell's detachment and now lives on Saline Creek. She states she was rudely forced from home by the soldiers where she left every article charged in the account and was never suffered to return.[153]

153 Marybelle W. Chase, *1842 Cherokee Claims, Saline District* (from originals located at the Tennessee State Library and Archives, Nashville, Tennessee), 54.

Daniel S. Butrick

Missionary,

Brainerd Mission, Tennessee

May 26, 1838

As the soldiers advanced towards a … house, two little children fled in fright to the woods. The woman pleaded for permission to seek them, or wait till they came in, giving positive assurances that she would then follow on, and join the company. But all entreaties were in vain; and it was not will a day or two after that she would get permission for one of her friends to go back after the lost children.[154]

154 Daniel S. Butrick, *The Journal of Rev. Daniel S. Butrick, May 19, 1838 – April 1, 1839* (Park Hill: The Trail of Tears Association, Oklahoma Chapter, 1998), 1-2.

James Simmons

Related by Belle Kendick Abbott

Pickens County

The Hon. James Simmons, of Pickens county, now 85 years of age, lived for many years among the Cherokee before they went away. He traded with them and said they were remarkable for paying their debts. He thought them a very kind, friendly people and did no harm, only in retaliation. He lived in seven miles of Talona (Saunders Town)...

Mr. Simmons was a justice of the peace at the time the order was issued for their removal. The first step toward this was an order from Governor Lumpkin requiring their firearms to be taken away. In pursuance of this order Mr. Simmons said they begged so piteously to keep their guns that he would have resigned his commission rather than obeyed this order, and thus caused them such sorrow. He let them all keep their guns that came under his control. There was a family of Ridges living near Mr. Simmons when the order for removal came. When Ridge heard of it he ran up the mountain and laid down in a huckleberry patch and laid his gun across his breast. "Don't touch me or I'll kill you," he said when they found him there. Mr. Simmons persuaded him to surrender and offered to go to the fort with him. Ridge surrendered and turned to Mr. Simmons for protection when he saw how the troops devastated his house. "Lieutenant, don't let the troops destroy these things," interposed Mr. Simmons, at which kindly intervention Ridge sighed deeply. On starting to the fort with Ridge's family the soldiers made him trot before them. Mr. Simmons, sorry for him, took him up on his horse behind him. The soldiers, some of them, he thought, treated the Indians very unkindly. One old woman, who walked too slow for them, they punched along with their bayonets. Finally, they put her on a horse, from which she fell off and was nearly killed. The next day after the Ridges' family went to the fort, Mr. Simmons visited them in their quarters. There he found one of his daughters writing a letter with a chicken feather pen and using a kind of ink made from barks. At his entrance she held up two fingers to him. By this signal he soon learned that she wanted two more days....She was writing the letter and asked Simmons finish it for her and also to intercede with them for her…

This he did, and obtained it. Mr. Simmons bought many of their ponies and cows and calves as they were leaving, and paid them the money for them. A pony was worth from $15 to $40; a cow and calf $8.50. At one time he had fifty milch cows in his lot that he bought from them. They bartered their wares with him for goods — deer skins, hams, baskets, pots, peltry, roots, herbs, etc. Most of the Indians hated to go away. When Two-dropper came to tell Mr. Simmons goodbye he cried like a child… The Indians in this section were all carried to Talking Rock Fort, in now Pickens county.[155]

155 *The Atlanta Constitution*, Nov. 24, 1889.

Peggy Fallingpot

Cherokee Nation citizen

For 3 Horses $1.20 $1.10 $1. $3.30

" 7 cows and calves @ $12 1 steer $9 93

" 20 head Stock Hogs @ 2. 40.

" 10 Sheep @ 3 $30.

" 1 House Crib & Stable 100.

" 10 acres cleared land @ $10 100.

" 1 Bed & furniture 10....

" 2 Ploughs @ 2 per 4.

" 1 pr Ploughing gear 4.

" 2 Dishes and small (crockery?) 2.

" 4 Pots, suit knives & forks 6....

" 1 Wheel & (?) cards 4.

" 1 Loom $3 1 Table 4 7.

" 1 cupboard 2.

" 1 (Bell?) 1.50

" 2 axes @ $2 cotton $2 $6 $42.50

The claimant in this case states (on oath) that she lives near Dirt Town & came to this country in Taylor's detachment now lives on Saline Creek. She states that everything charged in this account was left by her at her House when she was forced from home by the soldiers, that she was not permitted to take her bedding but was rudely forced away by the armed men, she found no valuation of her place at Fort Gibson. [156]

156 Marybelle W. Chase, *1842 Cherokee Claims, Saline District* (from originals located at the Tennessee State Library and Archives, Nashville, Tennessee), 53.

Daniel S. Butrick

Missionary,

Brainerd Mission, Tennessee

May 26, 1838

A man deaf and dumb, being surprised at the approach of armed men, attempted to make his escape, and because he did not hear and obey the command of his pursuers, was shot dead on the spot.[157]

---

157 Daniel S. Butrick, *The Journal of Rev. Daniel S. Butrick, May 19, 1838 – April 1, 1839* (Park Hill: The Trail of Tears Association, Oklahoma Chapter, 1998), 2.

N. W. Pittman

Daniel's Madison Company

From a letter written to his wife and family

A relation of actions taken on May 28, 1838

In the evening we the Madison company traveled taking Indian prisoners until midnight. Very much fatigued we encampt with some Indians whom we had taken prisoners. Some of us lay in the road, some in a house with the red people, the balance in another house [where] we had taken an Indian and his wife, and placed them all together. Some occupied the Indian bed before it was cold, and some under the same. The balance stretched on the floor until there was no room for any more. So taking our rest and slumber through the balance of the night. On the approach of morn we arose from our slumber, left a guard with our prisoners, then commenced our march from house to house, taking the red brethren and leaving guards at the different posts until we were all pretty well posted as guards.[158]

158 Letter to Henchin Strickland of Danielsville, Madison County, Ga., from his son-in-law, N.W. Pittman, and son H.P. Strickland, Series 1. Papers, 1838-1954, in the John R. Peacock papers #1895-z, Southern Historical Collection, The Wilson Library, University of North Carolina at Chapel Hill. http://finding-aids.lib.unc.edu/01895/

Daniel S. Butrick

Missionary

Brainerd Mission

One man it is said, had shot a deer, and was taking it home to meet the joyful calculations of his family, when at once he was surprised & taken prisoner to a fort.

Women absent from their families on visits, or for other purposes, were seized, and men far from their wives and children, were not allowed to return, and also children being forced from home, were dragged off among strangers. Cattle, horses, hogs, household furniture, clothing and money not with them when taken were left. And it is said that the white inhabitants around, stood with open arms to seize whatever property they could put their hands on. Some few who had friends to speak for them, were assisted afterwards in getting some part of their lost goods.[159]

159 Daniel S. Butrick, *The Journal of Rev. Daniel S. Butrick, May 19, 1838 – April 1, 1839* (Park Hill: The Trail of Tears Association, Oklahoma Chapter, 1998), 2.

Cricket Sixkiller

Island Town

Chattooga County, Georgia

May, 1838

Cherokee Nation

Going Snake District

Personally came before me Jesse Bushyhead Chief Justice of the Inferior Court of the Cherokee Nation Six Killer, who being duly qualified Testifies and says: In 1813 or 1814 I resided at Broom's Town on Chattooga. About two hundred troops of the United States were camped in the vicinity for some time, waiting to go on to the Creek War. My hogs were enticed to the camp by the wastage in the feeding of horses. I endeavored to get them away but could not. On the departure of the troops I went to camp and found the entrails of the slaughtered hogs scattered all about, and found sixty hogs missing from my stock. I have never received any compensation from any source.

A second company of troops on their way from Tennessee to the Creek War took forcibly from my corn crib forty bushels of corn which was selling at one dollar a bushel.

In 1838 I resided in Island Town on Chatoogi where myself and family were captured by the troops under the command of Major General Scott. (The property specified under that date in the foregoing schedule excepting the five dollars paid to Sawyer John, the Expense of removal from Camp Ross and the ten dollars of which I was defrauded.) were all left behind on my being captured by the Troops, and for which I have received no compensation from the proceeds of sales by the Commissioners of Indian property or from any other source. The facts concerning the ten dollars fraud are these. Capt. Jefferson Caldwell, an officer of the volunteers stationed in the Nation, left some saddles at my home to be safe. On one occasion he borrowed of me ten dollars, but left one saddle at my house. From that time I never saw him till I met him at Ross' Landing after my capture. I then bought the saddle of him & paid for it. I then asked him for the ten dollars but he refused to pay it without assigning any reason for his refusal.

In the spring of 1836, a man professing to be the Drawer in the Georgia Land Lottery was about to take away a part of my field, affirming it to be his property. I applied to Sawyer John who prevented him from doing so, for which I paid said John five dollars.

In regard to the removal from Ross' Landing, the facts are these. Myself and friends being prisoners wished to make the camp near the Agency the place of starting to the West. We obtained permission from Col. Lindsey, the officer in command, to remove. I hired a wagon of one Vann, a Cherokee, for which I paid $7.75 and it cost for provision for part of three day ten dollars and twenty five cents.

The forty-nine acres of land for which rent is charged formed a part of my field and a man named Jackson claimed it as Drawer, and was put in possession of it by the Georgia Guard. The Land was measured by Jackson himself.

Sworn to and submitted

Before me this 2nd of March 1842

Jesse Bushyhead

ChiefJustice Ct.

Six Killer his x mark

To Cricket Six Killer late of Island Town Chatoogi Cherokee Nation East. Removed in Daniel Cabon's detachment, now of Going Snake District.

116 head of hogs $348

1 Sorrel Mare and Colt $40

1 Grey horse $25

($413)

1 Bay Mare $20

100 Bushels Corn $100

800 Bushels Fodder $24

($144)

30 Grown Ducks $7.50

30 young $3.75

3 pots $5

($19.25)

(more stuff I can enumerate separately…)

Rent of one House taken forcible possession of by Walker Thornton and used by him three years

For this district Cricket Sixkiller who being duly qualified states I resided at Island Town on Chatoogi in 1838 when myself and family were captured by the troops of the United States under the command of General Scott. The items of property in the foregoing schedule were left behind on my capture and I have never received any compensation for any part of them from the proceeds of sales of the Commissioners of Indian property or from any other source.

The house for which I claim rent was the dwelling house of myself and family. In the year 1838 Walker Thornton came there and entered while I was gone to my father's one morning. When I returned I found him with his family and furniture in the house. He refused to give it up, affirming that the place was his as Drawer in the Georgia Land Lottery.

Sworn to and subscribed before me

This 2rd day of March, 1842

David M. Foreman

Cricket Six Killer his x Mark

Walker R. Thornton, Fleming's Franklin. Fourth Section, Sixth District, land lot 149.

On the Brainerd Road.

Six Killer being duly qualified states that he lived about a mile from the above named Cricket Sixkiller was well acquainted with his stock and property. The description of the principal items I know to be precisely correct. The stock of hogs and all the smaller particulars were such no induces me to believe the foregoing account to be correct statement of them.

Sometime in 1838 Cricket Sixkiller was at my house word was brought that a white man had taken possession of his house. I went with him to the house and found said Walker Thornton with his family and furniture in the house, and part of Cricket Sixkiller's things moved out into the Entry. We had a long talk with him but failed to get him to give up the house.

Sworn to and subscribed before me

This 3rd day of March 1842

David M. Foreman

Six Killer his x Mark.[160]

160 From a photographic copy of a claim made in 1842 in the *Goingsnake District* of the Cherokee Nation, provided by Michael Wren (from an original at the Gilcrease Museum Archives in Tulsa, Oklahoma).

A.R. Hetzel

Quartermaster

May 29, 1838

Indians collected at Fort Cumming under the orders of Genl. Scott will be considered in the light of prisoners of war and transportation for the baggage will be furnished by the quartermaster.[161]

161 Sarah H. Hill, *Cherokee Removal from Georgia*, 2005 (Original document at National Archives RG 92 Entry 350 Box 2 Vol. 2).

Daniel S. Butrick

Missionary

Thus in two or three days about 8,000 people, many of whom were in good circumstances, and some rich, were rendered homeless, houseless and penniless, and exposed to all the ills of captivity.

In driving them a platoon of soldiers walked before and behind, and a file of soldiers on each side, armed with all the common appalling instruments of death; while the soldiers, it is said would often use the same language as if driving hogs, and goad them forward with their bayonets.

One man, on being pricked thus, and seeing his children thus goaded on, picked up a stone and struck a soldier; but for this he was handcuffed, and on arriving at the fort, was punished and on starting again was whipped a hundred lashes.[162]

162 Daniel S. Butrick, *The Journal of Rev. Daniel S. Butrick, May 19, 1838 – April 1, 1839* (Park Hill: The Trail of Tears Association, Oklahoma Chapter, 1998), 2.

James Mooney

Myths of the Cherokee (1891)

"The Legend of Tsali"

One old man named Tsali, "Charley," was seized with his wife, his brother, his three sons and their families. Exasperated at the brutality accorded his wife, who, being unable to travel fast, was prodded with bayonets to hasten her steps, he urged the other men to join with him in a dash for liberty. As he spoke in Cherokee the soldiers, although they heard, understood nothing until each warrior suddenly sprang upon the one nearest and endeavored to wrench his gun from him. The attack was so sudden and unexpected that one soldier was killed and the rest fled, while the Indians escaped to the mountains. Hundreds of others, some of them from the various stockades, managed also to escape to the mountains from time to time, where those who did not die of starvation subsisted on roots and wild berries until the hunt was over. Finding it impracticable to secure these fugitives, General Scott finally tendered them a proposition, through (Colonel) W. H. Thomas, their most trusted friend, that if they would surrender Charley and his party for punishment, the rest would be allowed to remain until their case could be adjusted by the government. On hearing of the proposition, Charley voluntarily came in with his sons, offering himself as a sacrifice for his people. By command of General Scott, Charley, his brother, and the two elder sons were shot near the mouth of Tuckasegee, a detachment of Cherokee prisoners being compelled to do the shooting in order to impress upon the Indians the fact of their utter helplessness. From those fugitives thus permitted to remain originated the present eastern band of Cherokee.[163]

---

163 James Mooney, *History, Myths, and Sacred Formulas of the Cherokees* (Asheville: Bright Mountain Books, 1992) 131. http://www.learnnc.org/lp/editions/nchist-newnation/4547

Daniel S. Butrick

Missionary

Thursday, May 31

Just before night a young lieutenant called and requested accommodation for two or three officers, and permission for a company of Cherokees to camp near. Though we are not in the habit of entertaining any white men, yet for the sake of the poor Cherokees we worked to accommodate the above officers.

Astoundingly a little before sunset a company of about two hundred Cherokees were driven into our lane. The day had been rainy, and of course all men, women and children were dripping wet, with no change of clothing, and scarcely a blanket fit to cover them. As some of the women when taken from their houses, had on their poorest dress, this of course was the amount of their clothing for a journey of about eight hundred miles. As soon as permission was obtained from the officers, we opened every door to these poor sufferers. Mothers brought their dear little babes to our fire, and stripped off their only covering to dry.

O how heart rending was the sight of those little sufferers, their little lips blue and trembling with cold, seemed yet form a smile of gratitude for this kind reception. We wept and wept again, and still wept at the thought of that affecting scene. Our prayer is that these dear children, who must doubtless be soon ushered into eternity, may be taken into the arms of their Redeemer.

In the company were one or two blind men, and several persons unwell. One poor old Creek, being sick and wet was nourished by our fire.

A little before dark, the Capt. took an interest and went to those at the meeting house and told them he had the power to destroy them, and was ordered to do so if they did not behave well. He then told them that after the drum beat should beat, no one must be seen out doors till morning. His interpreter told him that some might be obliged to go out, having the dysentery. The Capt. replied that in that case they must call, and ask permission or they would be in danger of being shot.[164]

164 Daniel S. Butrick, *The Journal of Rev. Daniel S. Butrick, May 19, 1838 – April 1, 1839* (Park Hill: The Trail of Tears Association, Oklahoma Chapter, 1998), 2-3.

Order No. 16

General Charles Floyd

June 1, 1838

The Brig. Genl. Commanding the Mid Mily Dist. has been informed that an Indian was killed on the 28th May by Private (Frances M. Cuthbert) of Capt Cook's company, stationed at Fort Means. It seems by the official reports made to the Brig Genl on the subject, by the Commanding Officer at Fort Means and Capt Cook, that the Indian after having been captured, attempted to escape with some indications of hostility, and in consequence was shot by the soldier. The circumstances as communicated to the Brig Genl justify the act, and the subject is thus noticed in orders, not only to place in its true colour before the Georgia troops, that the soldier may not suffer any censure which a misunderstanding of the case might produce, but to prevent hereafter any unnecessary acts of violence for the justification of which this case might be referred to as precedent. It will be recollected by the officers and soldiers of the Georgia Brigade, that we are not in a state of war with the Cherokee Indians; that they have not committed any act of violence; that they are moving peaceably out of the Country, and that it will be honorable to the State, and highly advantageous to her Citizens, and particularly to those residing in the Cherokee Country to remove them without bloodshed. Their unresisting compliance with the orders to remove, and the sacrifices of property (and in many cases of feeling) which they must necessarily make, should render them objects of protection rather than abuse, among brave men. It is hereby ordered, that during the peaceable removal of the Indians, the troops within the Mid Mily Dist, will not use their weapons against the Indians, unless the latter assault or resist with deadly weapons when summoned to surrender, or attempt to escape from the custody of the Military. Forbearance in all cases be exercised consistently with the duties assigned to the soldiers. The Commanders of the several Posts, in the Mid: Mily: Dist: will promulgate their orders to the troops under their Command, respectively.[165]

165 John W. Latty, *Carrying Off the Cherokee* (Self-published, 2011), 110 (Original document: Order No. 16, Document 2009.003.0934, King Collection, Museum of the Cherokee Indian).

Stephen Foreman

Cherokee Nation Citizen

Candy's Creek Mission Station, Tennessee

From a letter to Rev. David Greene

May 31, 1838

From the date of my letter you will perceive that I am still in the Cherokee Nation East, and still in the neighborhood of Candy's Creek Missionary Station. Indeed, I am now living on the mission premises at C. Creek, and have been since Dec. last. How much longer we shall be permitted (to) remain here in our own lands, to enjoy our rights and privileges, I do not know. From the present aspect of affairs, we shall very soon be without house & home. Indeed, ever since the 23rd of May, we have been looking almost daily for the soldiers to come, and turn us out of our houses. They have already warned us to make preparations, and to come in to camps, before we were forced to do so. But I have stated distinctly to some of the officers at Head Quarters, what I thought of this, so called treaty, and what course I intended to persue in the event no new treaty was made, and see no reasons yet why I should change my mind. My determination, and the determination of a large majority of Cherokees, yet in the Nation is never to recognize this fraudulent instrument as a treaty, nor remove under it until we are forced to do so at the point of a bayonet. It may seem unwise and hazardous to the fraimers and friends of this instrument, that we should persue such a course, but I am fully satisfied it is the only one we can persue with clear consciences...

I shall also try to send you something every week following in either the shape of a letter or journal, until this critical time with us has passed, or until we arrive at the west, where it has been the wish and policy of the Govt. for a number of years, to deposit us. In the mean time, I hope the Com. and all our friends at the north will remember us constantly at the throne of grace. If any people ever needed the prayers and sympathies of Christians, it is the distressed and oppressed Cherokees.

S. Foreman[166]

166 Julia Coates, *Trail of Tears* (Santa Barbara: ABC-CLIO, 2014), 199-200.

Stephen Foreman

Cherokee Nation citizen

Candy's Creek Mission Station, Tennessee

From a postscript to a letter to Rev. David Greene

June 2, 1838

P.S. Five armed soldiers rode up, alighted & came into the house to let us know that we must be ready by Tuesday, the 5th inst. to go to Ross' landing. About all the Cherokees in the limits of Ga. are now collected into forts. I hope we shall all go peaceably when we are forced away. I hear of none resisting, but some being very much abused.

In haste,

S. Foreman[167]

---

167 Ibid.

Tawney

Cherokee Nation citizen

Candy's Creek, Tennessee

In the summer of 1838 I was forcibly compelled to leave (everything) except the horses and hogs and they were stolen, stolen by citizens of the United States, as I saw the white people driving them off and that I have good reason to believe they were also stolen by the whites and that all the balance I left in the Old Nation at the time I was forcibly compelled to leave home in the summer of 1838 in consequence of being arrested by the troops under the command of Genl. Scott and further I was never permitted to go back to my residence to get my property or dispose of the same and therefore I left every item…[168]

168 Marybelle W. Chase, *1842 Cherokee Claims, Flint District,* Vol. 3, Claim No. 112 (from originals located at the Tennessee State Library and Archives, Nashville, Tennessee), 343-344.

Sti chy

Cherokee Nation citizen

For property abandoned in the Eastern Nation, on the waters of Chatooga River, near the residence of D. Vann. Emigrated to this Country in 1838 in Old Fields' Detachment…

For Cash left in his house $400

" 1 Trunk $4.50 1 Saddle $25 29.50

" 4 Horses $320 1 coal $12 332.

" 1 pr Saddle Bags 5.

" 20 acres cleared land @ $10 200. — $966.50

The claimant states on oath that he lost this cash and every article charged in this account by being forcibly removed from home by the military, and that no chance has ever been afforded him of getting any thing for it.[169]

---

169 Marybelle W. Chase, *1842 Cherokee Claims, Saline District* (from originals located at the Tennessee State Library and Archives, Nashville, Tennessee), 222.

From the Editor

May 29, 1838

Apprehensions which were felt everywhere now have subsided. The militia companies stationed at this place and in this vicinity received their orders to collect the Indians; and without any delay, and with praiseworthy dispatch, on Sunday morning commenced their line of march. The Indians were at home and cheerfully obeyed the orders of the officers and prepared at once to take up their residence at Ft. Means, which was prepared to receive and detain them until further orders from Gen. Scott should be received. The Indians, finding that their time had arrived for their removal, in many instances did not remain ontheir farms to be carried to the fort by the troops but voluntarily come in, in large numbers. Last night two hundred and fifty Indians slept quietly in the fort — nearly, if not all the Cherokees in this neighborhood. The war with the Cherokees — which the government has been anxiously providing against for months past, has been terminated in a single day. …Too much can not be said in commendation of the promptitude of General Scott in this matter. If the officers had delayed their collection for one week after right of occupancy had expired, we believe it would have encouraged them in acts of resistance to emigration. But both officers and men were impressed with their duty and responsibility and cheerfully performed it.[170]

---

170 *The Western Georgian*, May 29, 1838.

Daniel S. Butrick

Missionary,

Brainerd Mission, Tennessee

June 3, 1838

Most of our neighbors are now with us, going this evening or tomorrow to the camps, choosing to go in by themselves, rather than be driven in by soldiers; and though we held public worship, yet we were considerably interrupted. [171]

171 Daniel S. Butrick, *The Journal of Rev. Daniel S. Butrick, May 19, 1838 – April 1, 1839* (Park Hill: The Trail of Tears Association, Oklahoma Chapter, 1998), 3.

Elizabeth Thornton

Cherokee Nation citizen

When I came to this country, the year the colera was so fatal among the Cherokee emigrants — and … on that account I put all my articles in charge of officers of the United States...to bring to Fort Gibson...which was never done — ...I lost every article of it…[172]

172 Marybelle W. Chase, *1842 Cherokee Claims, Saline District*, (from originals located at the Tennessee State Library and Archives, Nashville, Tennessee), 215.

Daniel S. Butrick

Missionary

Monday, June 11, 1838

Went to the camps… Inquired for Soft Shell Turtle but as his tent was some distance off, I did not visit him. He is a chief of some note, from Hightower.

When the soldiers were taking the people, he, with nearly thirty others, fled to a mountain. They were discovered a few days ago, and brought to the camps. He was handcuffed, and his hands considerably swollen when he came last week…

The weather being extremely warm and dry, many of the Cherokees are sick, especially at Calhoun, where we understand that from four to ten die in a day.[173]

173 Daniel S. Butrick, *The Journal of Rev. Daniel S. Butrick, May 19, 1838 – April 1, 1839* (Park Hill: The Trail of Tears Association, Oklahoma Chapter, 1998), 5.

Capt. James Word

A letter to Georgia Gov. George Gilmer

June 18, 1838

Five days passed and largely the rise of two hundred Indians were captured, without loss of life or the fire of a gun. As soon as a sufficient transportation could be had, those prisoners were marched to Ross' Landing, accompanied with a proper escort under the command of Lt. Rogers… After the above detachment had left for Ross' Landing I succeeded in capturing ten others, and sent them to New Echota and turned them over to the officer commanding at that post. I am of the opinion that we are now clear of the Cherokees in this part of the country, unless it be some few, who are land holders and have obtained certificates, entitling them to remain...[174]

---

174 Sarah H. Hill, "Fort Campbell GA Site Report," submitted to the Georgia Department of Natural Resources Historic Preservation Division in 2005, 17-18.

Evan Jones

Baptist missionary to the Cherokees

June 16, 1838

Well-furnished houses were left a prey to plunderers, who, like hungry wolves, follow in the trail of the captors. These wretches rifle the houses, and strip the helpless, unoffending owners of all they have on earth....a painful sight. The property of many has been taken and sold before their eyes for almost nothing – the sellers and buyers in many cases having combined to cheat the poor Indians. These things are done at the instant of arrest… the soldiers standing by, with their arms in hand, impatient to go on with their work, could give little time to transact business. The poor captive, in a state of distressing agitation, his weeping wife almost frantic with terror, surrounded by a group of crying, terrified children, without a friend to speak a consoling word, is in a poor condition to make a good disposition of his property and is in most cases stripped of the whole, at one blow. Many of the Cherokees, who, a few days ago, were in comfortable circumstances, are now victims of abject poverty. Some, who have been allowed to return home, under passport, to inquire after their property, have found their cattle, horses, swine, farming-tools, and house-furniture all gone. And this is not a description of extreme cases. It is altogether a faint representation of the work which has been perpetrated on the unoffending, unarmed and unresisting Cherokees.[175]

---

175 Theda Perdue and Michael D. Green, *The Cherokee Removal with Documents* (Boston: Bedford, 2005), 172.

William Jasper Cotter

White resident of Rock Spring,

near Coosawattee

A Remembrance

I had a part in all this tragic scene. Col. W. J. Howard, the quartermaster, boarded with us and kept his office in the Harlan house. There were no army wagons and teams, and he hired what he needed and gave father the privilege of furnishing some of the supplies for the post. Horses and oxen did most of the work. We had a yoke, strong and true, and they walked nearly as fast as horses. I was the driver.... In hauling the stuff from the cabins a file of six or more men went with me as a guard. They forced open the doors and put the poor, meager household effects into the wagons, sometimes the stuff of two or three families at one load. After following me a mile or two the guards galloped away, leaving me in worse danger than any one else; for if there had been an Indian hiding out, I would have been the one to suffer.

But few of the Indians ever went back to their homes. We turned the cows and calves together, as they had been apart a day or two. Chickens, cats, and dogs all ran away when they saw us. Ponies under the shade trees fighting the flies with the noise of their bells; the cows and calves lowing to each other; the poor dogs howling for their owners; the open doors of the cabins as we left them – to have seen it all would have melted to tenderness a heart of stone. And in contrast there was a beautiful crop of corn and beans.[176]

176 William Jasper Cotter, *My Autobiography* (Nashville: Publishing House Methodist Episcopal Church, South, 1917), 39-40 https://archive.org/details/myautobiographycc00cott

Uk kwahle

Cherokee Nation citizen

For 1 House and 8 acres cleared land 180.

" 1 stable 25$ 8 Peach trees 8. 33.

" 4 head Horses @ $100 $400.

" 1 cow & calf, 1 yr old steer & yearling 30

" 27 Head stock hogs @ 2. 54

" 3/4 of an acre in Sweet Potatoes 20…

" 1 " " do " " cotton 10

" 1 Pot $4 1 do 2.50$ 6.50

" 1 Bed Stead 4.00

" 1 Table $4. — 1 Spinning Wheel $4 8.00

" 4 Chairs 2.25 9 Plates 2.50 4.75

" 1 set k & forks .75

" 2 M Weavers Harness @ 2.50 5.00

" 1 Slay $1 5th clean cotton 1.25 2.25

" 30 (symbol) seed cotton @ 4 ¢ 1.20

" 1 Sifter 75 ¢ 12 chickens @ 12 1/2 ¢ 2.25

" 1 Pad Lock 1.00

777.70

The claimant in this case states (on oath) that she lived on Cedar Creek in the old nation, and that she came to this country with a company that was forced off, by the way of the River, under U.S. agents and now lives on Spring Creek. She states that she was forced from home by the soldiers and driven to the boat to come to this country, and that all the property in the account was left, and lost to her, never having since heard from it. That she sent her brother Henry Earbob to Fort Gibson to inquire whether the place had ever been valued, who could find no account of it on the Books.[177]

---

177 Marybelle W. Chase, *1842 Cherokee Claims, Saline District* (from originals located at the Tennessee State Library and Archives, Nashville, Tennessee), 16.

General Nathaniel Smith

Superintendent of Cherokee Removal

From a letter to Tennessee county agents

I have appointed you Agents to act jointly for the purpose of collecting and selling the personal effects of the Cherokee Indians ... after the Indians are removed from their present locations, by military force. The property to be collected and sold by you embraces every thing of a personal and moveable nature to which any value whatever can be attached ...[178]

178 Office of Indian Affairs, M234, Roll #115

Daniel S. Butrick

Missionary

June 10, 1838

By permission we attempted to hold a meeting at the camps. On the way we passed a company of nearly 1,000 poor Cherokee prisoners, under a formidable guard of soldiers…

About noon we collected a few, and spent sometime in prayer. Not long however, after commencing, we were interrupted by the arrival of another company of prisoners, consisting of about 1,000.

As we were leaving the camps we found a woman lying senseless. On her arrival today, being unwell, she was not able to endure the sight of some friends she saw in the camps, and immediately on seeing them, she fainted and fell to the ground.

When the company was driven from Lafayette, one woman fainted and fell in the road, as she was driven on.

Another in the company, being seized with the pains of childbirth, stopped with her mother an hour or so, and then with her child, assisted by her aged mother went on to overtake her friends.

On returning to Brainerd, the reflections and occurances of the day seemed overwhelming, Groaning was my only repast. It seemed a luxury to groan and weep…

The Cherokees had been kept on a small spot, surrounded by a strong guard, under such circumstances it would seem impossible for male or female to secrete themselves from the gaze of multitudes for any purpose whatever, unless by hanging up some cloth in their tents, and there they had no vessel for private use.

…(I)t is evident that from their first arrest they were obliged to live much like brute animals, and during their travels, were obliged at night to lie down on the naked ground, in the open air, exposed to wind and rain, and herd together, men women and children, like droves of hogs, and in this way, many are hastening to a premature grave.

Half the infants six months or a year and all the aged over sixty had been killed directly, and one fourth of the remainder, and the residue suffered to continue under favorable circumstances till they could move with safety, a vast amount of expense and suffering would apparently have been saved, and as many lives, or nearly as many, have been spared to witness the returns of another year as will now. Driving them under such circumstances, and then forcing them into filthy boats, to overflowing in this hot season, landing them at Little Rock, a most sickly place, to wait other means of conveyance 200 miles up the Arkansas river, is only a most expensive and painful way of putting the poor people to death...[179]

179 Butrick, Daniel S., *The Journal of Rev. Daniel S. Butrick, May 19, 1838 – April 1, 1839* (Park Hill: The Trail of Tears Association, Oklahoma Chapter, 1998), 6.

Evan Jones

Baptist missionary to the Cherokees

July 10, 1838

The overthrow of the Cherokee Nation is completed. The whole population are made prisoners.[180]

180 William G. McLoughlin, *Champions of the Cherokees: Evan and John B. Jones* (Princeton: Princeton University Press, 1990), 176.

‘Into the boats, under guard’

Lt. Edward Deas

Cherokee Removal, June 1838

Journal Of Occurrences on the Route of Emigration of a Party of Cherokees from Ross' Landing E. Tenn.eto Fort Coffee Ark...

6th June 1838

The present party of Cherokees consists mostly of Indians that were collected by the Troops and inhabited that portion of the Cherokee country embraced within the limits of the state of Georgia, and were assembled at Ross' Landing E. Tenne preparatory to setting out upon the Journey.

The number of the Party is about six hundred, but is not yet accurately known, as it was thought inexpedient to attempt to make out the muster rolls before starting. The Indians were brought into the boats under guard & being necessary somewhat crowded, any unnecessary delay while in that situation was by all means to be avoided on account of the health of the people. It was therefore thought best to set out from the points of assembly without waiting to muster the Party, leaving it to be done by the conductor after starting, when more accurate books could probably be made than before setting out.

The route related by the Superintendent is by water, and the Party was turned over to me to-day at Ross' Landing, after having been placed on board of the Boats provided for its transportation at Decatur Ala.a

These consist of a small S. Boat of about 100 Tons burthern, and 6 Flat-Boats, one with double cabins (one upon the other) of a large size. The others are middle sized Boats, but appointed by capacity to transport the Party without being too much crowded.

The Boats having been lashed side by side, 3 on each side of the Steam Boat, all were got under way about noon and proceeded at about 4 or 5 miles an hour, until we arrived near the Suck when it was necessary to separate them in passing throu' the mountains. The Suck, Boiling-Pot, the Skillet, and the Frying-Pan are names given to the different rapids formed in the Tennessee Basin as it passes through the Cumberland Mountains.

The river here follows a very circuitous course, a distance of 80 miles by water being only equal to 8 by land.

The Suck is the first and most difficult and dangerous of the rapids. The river here becomes very narrow and swift with the Banks on either side are rocky and steep, it being the point at which the stream passes thru' a gorge in the mountains. The S. boat with one Flat on each side passed thro' with most of the people on board, but after getting thro' the most rapid water, it was found impossible to keep her in the channel, & in consequence was thrown upon the north Bank with some violence but luckily none of the people were injured although one of the Flats was a good deal smashed.

The other 4 boats came thro' two by two and the party was encamped before dark as it was too late in the day to reach the foot of the rapids in daylight.

The present party is accompanied by a guard of 23 men in order to prevent any desertions that might be attempted before leaving the limits of the Cherokee country.

7th June

The S. Boat and Flat Boats were got under weigh this morning and came thro' the remainder of the rapids. The first started at 8 o'clock, and all were got thro' by noon.

The boats having been lashed side by side they continued to proceed at the rate of from 4 to 5 miles an hour thro' the reminder of the day.

8th June

Last night being clear and the moon nearly at full the boats continued to run until near daylight this morning when they were obliged to stop and separate owing to the Fog which suddenly spring up.

We passed Gunter's Landing about 9 o'clock and then continued to run (stopping once for wood) until dark, when the Boats were landed for the night 6 miles above Decatur, and much of the people on shore have gone ashore to sleep and cook. The weather has been remarkably fine since starting and the people generally healthy though there are several cases of sickness amongst the children.

9th June

The Boats started this morning early and reached Decatur about 6 o'clock, but on arriving it was found that the Rail road cars were not in readiness although they had been notified that the party was approaching.

We have therefore been obliged to remain here to-day.

Two locomotives have arrived in readiness to transport the party to Tuscumbia tomorrow.

10th June

This morning early the Indians and their baggage were transferred from the Boats to the Rail Road cars. About 32 cars were necessary to transport the Party, and no more could be employed for want of power in the locomotive engines.

The Indians therefore being necessarily crowded, I determined not to take the guard any further, as I heard the Steam Boat Smelter was waiting their arrival at the other end of the Rail Road, and in that case there would be no necessity for the guard, as the party would embark without any delay at Tuscumbia. On the arrival of the 1st Train Cars at Tuscumbia landing about 3 o'clock PM. The Steamboat was in readiness and took nearly half the Party on board but immediately set-out for Waterloo at the foot of the Rapids without accounting for the 2nd train of cars with the remainder of the party. In consequence when the 2nd Train arrived between 4 & 5 o clock there being no boat to receive the remainder of the Party on board they were necessarily encamped near the S. Boat landing for the night, and tho' the guard having been sent back for the reasons above stated, and having no doubt that the Steam boat Smelter would remain, drunkenness and disorder may be expected to-night. Nothing could be more unfortunate than the departure of the Boat at the moment the Party was on the point of reaching here.

11th June

As might be expected there was much drunkenness in camp last night and over one hundred of the Indians deserted. The remainder were conveyed from Tuscumbia Landing to Waterloo (30 miles) on one of the double deck keels and a small steam boat.

The party was there established on board the Smelter and the two keels such as are described in the contract for transportation & about 2 o'clock these boats were got under weight and have since continued to run from 10 to 12 miles an hour.

As there is room enough on board to accommodate the party with sleeping room ... we shall continue to run thro' the night.

Until we reached Waterloo the rations consisted of flour corn meal, & bacon. At Tuscumbia yesterday I had purchased 4 day supply of fresh beef, but owing to the heat of the weather and the of the party most of it became spoiled and unfit for use, before it could be issue when the party was assembled on the Smelter today

<u>12th June</u>

The Boats continued to run until this forenoon at 1 o'clock (when a stop was made for wood) and reached Paducah between 4 & 5 P.M. I have enrolled the Party as accurately & carefully as possible since leaving Tuscumbia and find the number to be 489.

Finding that the S. Boat and one keel are sufficient to transport the party the other was left at Paducah this afternoon, and the rate of travelling is thereby much increased. We left Paducah about sun set and shall continue to sun thro' the night.

The weather since starting with the Party has been warm and as yet there had been no rain. The People have been generally healthy and then are but few cases of sickness at present and more of a dangerous character.

<u>13th June</u>

The Boats reached the mouth of the Ohio about midnight and have since continued to run stopping twice to wood in daylight. We passed Memphis this evening between 9 & 10 o'clock, but did not land. A small boat was and ashore to carry letters and procure provisions.

The weather continues warm but the night being clear and calm the boats will continue warm but the night being clear and calm the boats will continue to run. The people remain generally healthy.

14th June

The Boats continued to run last night and to day without interruption (except to wood in the forenoon) and reached Montgomery's Point at the mouth of White River at one o'clock PM

A pilot for the Arkansas R was then taken on board without landing, and we then entered White River passed thru' the cut-off into the Arkansas and continued to run until about sun set, having ascended the Arkansas about 70 miles. Most of the people have gone on shore and encamped for the night. The weather continues find tho' warm and the Party remains generally healthy. A small quantity of F. Beef was procured last-night at Memphis and was issued to-day.

The Arkansas River is low at present--a circumstance very unusual at this particular season of the year.

15th June

The boats got-under way this morning at sun-rise and continued to run through the day stopping once to wood in the forenoon. We stopped for the night at a wood landing at dark, having run to-day about 70 miles and many of the people have gone on shore and encamped for the night.

The weather continues warm and there has been slight rain thro' the day. The Arkansas continues very nearly at a stand.

16th June

It rained very hard last night for a short time. The boats got under weigh this morning at day light and this afternoon about sun set landed 14 miles below Little Rock.

The distance traveled today is about the same as yesterday not far from 70 miles.

A very perceptible rise has taken place in the River to-day and from the appearance of the water it is problem caused by the melting of snows. The weather continues warm.

17th June

We started this morning after sun-rise and reached Lt. Rock about 8 A.M. The S. Boat was anchored in the Stream a short time to prevent access to whiskey.

The river continues to rise and as we have to lie by generally at night, I determined to leave the Keel Boat and give the people the main cabin of the S. Boat instead.

Thereby we shall travel much faster, and there is at the same time room enough for them, by this arrangement.

We left Little Rock about 10 A.M. and continued to run until near sun-set, when we stopped for the nigh a few miles below Lewisbugh, and most of the people are now encamped on the shore. The weather continues fine and the Party healthy. The River continues to rise yesterday and today and this evening it appears to be at a stand.

18th June

We set-out this morning at daylight and continued to run with little interruption until dark, then stopped on the north bank opposite McLeans Bottom 2 miles above Titsworths' Place.

The people have gone above to sleep and prepare food. They still remain generally healthy.

The weather to-day was very warm. The river has fallen about a foot here, within the last 24 hours.

19th June

The People were got on board the boats and the boats started this morning between 2 & 3 o'clock, but had to stop again before daylight-on account of heavy rain. They were got under weigh again at light and continued to run until 10 A.M. when we were again obliged to land on account of a slight accident, to the wheel.

After 2 hours delay we again proceeded and … about 2 P.M. and stopped about an hour in the stream without landing the S. Boat.

We passed Fort Smith between 3 & 4 P.M. and reached Fort Coffee a little before sun-set.

The boats were landed opposite the Fort to procure food, and the people went on shore for the night as normal.

The weather continues extremely warm but the Party remains generally healthy.

Fort Coffee

20 June

After the Party landed last evening I found that they had taken all of their baggage out of the Boats and were desirous of stopping in this neighborhood.

The(y dervive) much pleasure at reaching their country in "safety" and meeting some of their friends and acquaintances here, and finding that others of them are living not far off, they prefer remaining here to proceeding to Fort Gibson.

I should have preferred to deliver them at the latter place, as there is water enough for the Boat to go up, at present; but at the same time considered it proper to consult their wishes.

After counseling together and with their friends from the vicinity they decided in favor of proceeding no further.

I therefore to-day discharged and paid ... the agents & physicians that accompanied the Party who returned on the S. Boat Smelter.

This morning early an express was dispatched by the Comandg Officer with a letter from myself to the officer at Fort Gibson appointed to receive the Cherokees, giving information that the Party is at this place, awaiting to be mustered and to receive their subsistence.

Fort Coffee

23rd June

Since arriving at this place I have issued a sufficient quantity of cotton to the Indians for tents to protect them from the weather. I have done so in consideration of their destitute Condition, as they were for the most part separated from their homes in Georgia, without having the means or time to prepare for camping and it was also the opinions of the Physicians of the Party that the health of these people would suffer if not provided with some protection from the weather.

Last evening an Agent of Capt. J.R. Stephenson the Disbg Agent to receive the Cherokees arrive this place and to-day I had the Party mustered in his presence. The number was found to be 489, as shown by the muster-roll, no deaths having occurred upon the journey and no alteration having taken place since the Party was enrolled.

The foregoing remarks embraced all matters of interest affecting the Indians, that came under my observation from the day of setting out upon the Journey until the Party was to-day turned over to the Agent appointed to muster & receive it.

Edw Deas Lieut U.S.A. Conductor[181]

181 Journal of Occurrences Of Lt. Edward Deas 1838, National Archives Record Group 574, Records of the Bureau of Indian Affairs, Special Case Files Of The Office of Indian Affairs 1807-1994, Roll 69, D235
http://ualrexhibits.org/trailoftears/eyewitness-accounts/journal-of-edward-deas-cherokee-removal-june-1838

'Divine indignation.'

John Ross

Letter to Major General Winfield Scott

Aquohee Camp

July 23, 1838

...The present condition of the Cherokee people is such that all dispute as to the time of emigration is set at rest. Being already severed from their homes & their property: their persons being under the absolute control of the Commanding General. And being altogether dependent on the benevolence & humanity of that high officer for the suspension of their transportation to the West at a season and under circumstances in which sickness and death were to be apprehended to an alarming extent, all inducements to prolong their stay in this country are taken away. And however strong their attachment to the homes of their fathers may be, their interests and their wishes now, are to depart as early as may be consistent with their safety...

We beg leave therefore very respectfully to propose: that the Cherokee Nation will undertake the whole business of removing their people to the West of the river Mississippi.[182]

---

182 Congressional Serial Set, Index to the Executive Documents, 25th Congress, 3d Session, 1838, 429.

Anonymous

Army and Navy Chronicle

October 25, 1838

FROM THE CHEROKEE COUNTRY. — Letters received in Norfolk from Athens, Tennessee, the present head quarters of Gen. Scott, dates Oct. 3d, state that the extensive drought had prevented the emigration of the Indians as contemplated, the rivers being low, and there not being water enough to sustain the Indians and their cattle. The emigration was thus retarded one month, but at our advices, showers of rain had fallen, and one thousand Indians were to have departed on the 2d for the west. At short intervals parties of 1,000 each would follow suit, and it is probable that at this time all the Indians are on their way westward, except the decrepit and sick, who will remain until the rivers become navigable.

Great praise is due to Gen. Scott for the patience and discretion displayed by him throughout the whole of this troublesome affair, and it is to his prudent foresight and prompt action that the country is exempt from a worse than Florida war.

We understand that the Indians are anxious to depart, and will move the alacrity, in spite of underhanded measures designed to work upon their feelings and render them dissatisfied and mutinous. — *Beacon.*[183]

---

183 *Army and Navy Chronicle*, October 25, 1838. http://ualrexhibits.org/trailoftears/indian-removal/cherokee-removal-chronicle-1830-1839/

Daniel S. Butrick

Missionary

Brainerd Mission Station

September 1, 1838

This is the day appointed for the Cherokees to commence their journey to the west, yet the drought is such that they cannot travel in large companies without great suffering for want of water.

The Chickamauga Creek is probably lower than it has ever been known to be by the oldest persons living.[184]

184 Daniel S. Butrick, *The Journal of Rev. Daniel S. Butrick, May 19, 1838 – April 1, 1839* (Park Hill: The Trail of Tears Association, Oklahoma Chapter, 1998), 33.

John Adair Bell

Treaty Party Detachment

From a letter written to Capt. John E. Page

October 2, 1838

Having understood from you… that you intended ordering only one wagon with five horses for every 20 persons in a detachment I have concluded to trouble you with this letter in the hope that I shall be able to convince you that something more than that ought to be done for us. You must be aware that 20 persons cannot be removed in comfort and safety in a single wagon as it would force us to put our women and children on foot and at the present and during the approaching season, such a course could not but be attended with sickness and great want of comfort…

By reference to the treaty, you will see that the government binds itself to furnish a sufficient number of wagons to remove us comfortably, without endangering our health, and at this season of the year and the still more inclement season approaching, this cannot be accomplished if 20 persons are only entitled to one wagon.[185]

185 Wayne Dell Gibson, "Cherokee Treaty Party Moves West: The Bell-Deas Overland Journey, 1838-1839," *The Chronicles of Oklahoma* 79 (Fall 2001): 322.

William Shorey Coodey

Cherokee Nation Citizen

From a letter written August 13, 1840,

Regarding a departing detachment to the West

The entire Cherokee population were captured by the U.S. troops under General Scott in 1838 and marched, to principally, upon the border of Tennessee where they were encamped in large bodies until the time for their removal west. At one of these encampments, twelve miles south of the Agency, and Head Quarters of Genl. Scott, was organised the first detachment for marching under the arrangement committing the whole management of the immigration into the hands of the Cherokees themselves.

The first of Septer. was fixed as the time for a part to be in motion on the route. Much anxiety was felt, and great exertions made by the Cherokees to comply with everything reasonably to be expected of them, and it was determined that the first detachment should move in the last days of August.

I left the Agency on the 27th, after night, and reached the encampment, above alluded to, early the following morning, for the purpose of aiding in the arrangements necessary to get a portion in motion on that day, the remainder to follow the next day and come up while the first were crossing the Tennessee River, about twenty five miles distant.

At noon all was in readiness for moving. The trains were stretched out in a line along the road through a heavy forest, groups of persons formed about each waggon, others shaking the hand of some sick friend of relative who would be left behind. The temporary camps covered with boards and some of bark, that for three summer months had been their only shelter and *home* were crackling and falling under a blazing flame. The day was bright and beautiful, but a gloomy thoughtfulness was strongly depicted in the lineaments of every face. In all the bustle of preparation there was a silence and stillness of the voice that betrayed the sadness of the heart.

At length the word was given to *move on*. I glanced along the line and form of Going Snake, an aged and respected chief whose head eighty winters had whitened, mounted on his favorite poney passed before me and lead the way in advance, followed by a number of young men on horse back.

At this very moment a low sound of distant thunder fell on my ear. In almost an exact western direction a dark spiral cloud was rising above the horizon and sent forth a murmur I almost fancied a voice of divine indignation for the wrongs of my poor and unhappy countrymen, driven by *brutal* power from all they loved and cherished in the land of their fathers, to gratify the cravings of avarice. The sun was unclouded — no rain fell — the thunder rolled away and seemed hushed in the distance. The scene around and before me, and in the elements above were peculiarly impressive & singular. It was at once spoken of by several persons near me, and looked upon as ominous of some future event in the West. In several letters written to my friends on the same evening I alluded to the circumstances, so strong was the effect on my own mind, at the time.[186]

186 http://freepages.genealogy.rootsweb.ancestry.com/~talbotfamilyhistory/11119.htm

Rebecca Neugin

Memories of the Trail

Related in 1932

My father had a wagon pulled by two spans of oxen to haul us in. Eight of my brothers and sisters and two or three widow women and children rode with us. My brother Dick, who was a good deal older than I was, walked along with a long whip which he popped over the backs of the oxen and drove them all the way. My father and mother walked all the way also.[187]

187 Rebecca Neugin, "Memories of the Trail." *Journal of Cherokee Studies* 3, no. 3 (1978): 46.

Capt. H. B. Henegar

Recollections

Related October 25, 1897

We crossed the Tennessee at the mouth of the Hiwassee, at Blythe's Ferry, went across Walden's Ridge to Pikeville, thence to McMinnville, thence over to Nashville. After crossing the river there we went to Hopkinsville, Kentucky, crossing the Ohio River at Golconda, thence through Southern Illinois to Green's Ferry, on the Mississippi. Our detachment was stopped twenty miles from the river, at Gore's encampment, for those ahead to get across the Mississippi. After the way was opened we went to the river and commenced to cross and were detained over three weeks...[188]

188 H. B. Henegar, "Recollections of the Cherokee Removal." *Journal of Cherokee Studies* 3, no. 3 (1978): 47.

Daniel S. Butrick

Missionary

November 26, 1838

...We traveled but about four miles from Nashville & camped.

As the fires began to be kindled, an aged Cherokee, who had been sick all the way, lay down by the fire, when his clothes caught fire, and he sprang up, but before he could be relieved, was burnt nearly to death.[189]

189 Daniel S. Butrick, *The Journal of Rev. Daniel S. Butrick, May 19, 1838 – April 1, 1839* (Park Hill: The Trail of Tears Association, Oklahoma Chapter, 1998), 47.

Daniel S. Butrick

Missionary

December 1, 1838

Camped on a branch of Red River, in Kentucky, having travelled during the week about 60 miles.

The poor old man who was burnt, was left in a house to be taken care of, but died in a few days.[190]

190 Ibid.

A Native of Maine. traveling in the Western Country

Special to the New York Observer

January 26, 1839

On Tuesday evening we fell in with a detachment of the poor Cherokee Indians — about eleven hundred Indians — sixty waggons — six hundred horses, and perhaps forty pairs of oxen. We found them in the forest camped for the night by the road side ... under a severe fall of rain accompanied by heavy wind. With their canvas a shield from the inclemency of the weather, and the cold west ground for a resting place, after the fatigue of the day, they spent the night ... many of the aged Indians were suffering extremely from the fatigue of the journey, and the ill health consequent upon it. Several were then quite ill, and one aged man we were informed was then in the last struggles of death.

About ten officers and overseers in each detachment ... was to provide supplies for the journey, and to attend to the general wants of the company... We met several detachments in the southern part of Kentucky on the 4th, 5th, and 6th of December. The last detachment which we passed on the 7th embraced rising two thousand Indians with horses and mules in proportion. The forward part of the train we found just pitching their tents for the night, and notwithstanding some thirty or forty waggons were already stationed, we found the road literally filled with the procession for about three miles in length. The sick and feeble were carried in waggons — about as comfortable for traveling as a New England ox cart with a covering over it — a great many ride on horseback and multitudes go on foot — even aged females, apparently nearly ready to drop into the grave, were traveling with heavy burdens attached to the back — on the sometimes frozen ground, and sometimes muddy streets, with no covering for the feet except what nature had given them. We were some hours making our way through the crowd, which brought us in close contact with the wagons and multitude, so much that we felt fortunate to find ourselves freed from the crowd without leaving any part of our carriage. We learned from the inhabitants on the road where the Indians passed, that they buried fourteen or fifteen at every stopping place, and they make a journey of ten miles per day only on an average. One fact which to my own mind seemed a lesson indeed to the American nation is, that they will not travel on the Sabbath... When the Sabbath came, they must stop, and not merely stop — they must worship the Great Spirit, too, for they had divine service on the Sabbath — a camp-meeting in truth.

One aged Indian who was commander of the friendly Creeks and Seminoles in a very important engagement in the company with General Jackson, was accosted on arriving in a little village in Kentucky by an aged man residing there, and who was one of Jackson's men in the engagement referred to, and asking him if he (the Indian) recollected him? The aged Chieftain looked him in the face and recognized him, and with a down-cast look and heavy sigh, referring to the engagement, he said "Ah! my life and the lives of my people were then at stake for you and your country. I then thought Jackson my best friend. But ah! Jackson no serve me right. Your country no do me justice now!"

The Indians as a whole carry in their countenances every thing but the appearance of happiness. Some carry a downcast dejected look bordering on the appearance of despair; others a wild frantic appearance as if about to burst the chains of nature and pounce like a tiger upon their enemies... Most of them seemed intelligent and refined. Mr. Bushyhead, son of an aged man of the same name, is a very intelligent and interesting Baptist clergyman. Several missionaries were accompanying them to their destination.[191]

191 *New York Observer*, Jan. 26, 1839

Martin Davis

A letter to his father, Daniel Davis

December 26, 1838

Mississippi River, Illinois

I take this opportunity to inform you I am well at present I ought to have wrote sooner but I have been in bad health ever since I passed Galconda, Ill. with the cramp colic but I have got entirely well You have no doubt heard by this time about the accident which happened to our Detachment in crossing the Ohio River at Galconda The ferry boat is carried by steam across the river vix the way of Berry's Ferry Well to hand the boat had reached the bank of the river and wagons and load taken off and starting back to the east bank for another load they had gotten about thirty yards from the west bank when the boiler burst and scalded a great many persons There were only two killed at all one a white man the other a cherokee. One was from our Detachment. This happened after I crossed the river in the evening.

On the morning following There is the coolest weather in Illinois I ever experienced anywhere The streams are all frozen over something like eight or twelve inches thick We are compelled to cut through the ice to get water for ourselves and animals it snows here every two or three days at the fartherest We are now camped in Missippi swamp four miles from the river and there is no possible chance of crossing the river for the numerous quantity of ice that comes floating down the river every day We have only traveled sixty five miles on the last month including the time spent at this place which has been about three weeks It is unknown when we shall cross the river it may be one month from this day which is the 26th of December 1838 I think we shall not reach Arkansas til March at least My oxen teams holds out extremely well at our low rate of travelling as they have now been worth $300.00 each including the hire of drivers I am unable to say what time I will be home I have issued six thousand pounds of beef and pork since I went in service of General Scott and in proportion of meal flour sugar coffee soap and salt That is to the ration 3 half pints meal or one pound flour per day per ration Four pounds of coffee and eight pounds sugar to every hundred rations Four qts of salt to every hundred rations and three pounds soap I have been able all the time to attend to business which is a greateal of trouble and very disagreeable in bad weather like it is at this time We have now but as to my heart I don't care if we don't reach Arkansas until next summer Christmas day passed without notice in this country I shall write oftener to all of you write me at Fort Gibson by the time you think I reach there Give my respects to all inquiring friends...[192]

192 Martin Davis and Mattie Lorraine Adams, *Family Tree of Daniel and Rachel Davis* (Duluth: Claxton Printing Company, 1973), 24.

Rebecca Neugin

Memories of the Trail

Related in 1932

The people got so tired of eating salt pork on the journey that my father would walk through the woods as we traveled, hunting for turkeys and deer which he brought into camp to feed us. Camp was usually made at some place where water was to be had and when we stopped and prepared to cook our food, other emigrants who had been driven from their homes without opportunity to secure cooking utensils came to our camp to use pots and kettles. There was so much sickness among the emigrants and a great many little children died of whooping cough.[193]

193 Rebecca Neugin, "Memories of the Trail." *Journal of Cherokee Studies* 3, no. 3 (1978): 46.

A Report from the *Arkansas Gazette*

November 8, 1838

Published February 6, 1839

Four detachments of the emigrating Cherokees have, within a few days, passed through our city, and seven others are behind, and are expected to pass in a week or two. They average about a thousand each. Of the third party, our brother Evan Jones, who has been eighteen years a missionary in the nation, is conductor; and the fourth is under the direction of the celebrated Dta-ske-ge-de-hee, known among us as Bushyhead. In the two parties they direct, we learn there are upwards of five hundred Baptists.

During two or three days, that their business detained them in the vicinity of this city, we have had the pleasure of some intercourse with these and others of our Cherokee brethren; and more lovely and excellent Christians we have never seen. On Monday evening last, the 5th of November, several of them were with us, at the monthly concert of prayer for missions. It was expected that the meeting would be addressed by Oganaya (Peter,) Ga-ne-tuh (John Wickliffe,) and the Chief, Sut-tu-a-gee, all in Cherokee, and interpreted by Dsa-gee. Some of these brethren, however, were sick, and others were detained by other causes, but their places were well supplied. We had a very crowded house. The services were commenced by singing a hymn in Cherokee, by brethren Jones, (who, by the way, is called by the Indians Ga-wo-hee-lo-ose-keh,) Dta-ske-ge-de-hee, Gha-nune-tdah-cla-gee (Going on the hill,) and Aht-zthee. After prayer, and another hymn, we were addressed by Ga-wo-he-lo-ose-keh, and Dta-ske-ge-de-hee, in English, and, in a very interesting manner, by Aht-zthee in Cherokee, interpreted by br. Bushyhead; and the services closed in the usual form. The effect was thrilling, and the people, though we did not ask a collection, spontaneously came up, and contributed to the Baptist mission among the Cherokees.

Last night, (the 7th,) br. Jones and br. Bushyhead were again with us. Two other Indian brethren, whose names we did not write down, and cannot remember, were expected, but the rain, which had been falling all day, in the evening poured down in torrents, and they did not come into the city. Our congregation was much larger than we expected. Br. Bushyhead addressed us in English, after prayer and a hymn in Cherokee, on the subject of missions. After pointing out the scripture authority and obligations to the holy work, he told us that he could very well remember when his nation knew nothing of Jesus Christ. He detailed to us some particulars in relation to their religious opinions, and method of spending their time, their habits, and domestic manners, and contrasted them with the present condition and character of his people, and thus illustrated the happy effects already produced among them by the gospel. He told us he recollected most distinctly the first time he ever heard the name of the Savior. He recounted to us some particulars of his conversion and that of his father and mother, and gave a short account of the effects of his own, and the preaching of Oganaya, and others, among his countrymen, and especially of the glorious revival that prevailed among them in their camps this summer, during which himself and Ga-ne-tuh and others had baptized over a hundred and seventy, upwards of fifty of whom were baptized on one occasion. He adverted to the opposition to missions waged by some Tennessee Baptists, and presented himself and hundreds of his brethren as living instances of the blessing of God upon missionary labors. He closed by stating that it was now seen that Cherokees could be Christians; commending his nation particularly, and the Indians generally to the prayers of the Lord's people, and beseeching them still to sustain the preaching of the gospel among them. He sat down in tears.

Br. Jones followed in a very eloquent address on the same subject, adding some interesting observations about the translation of the bible into Cherokee, in the letter invented by See-qua-yah (G. Guess,) at present in progress by himself and br. Bushyhead. The effect produced will not soon be erased from our mind, and we trust the recollection of the numerous instances recited of God's goodness and mercy to our red brethren, will add fervor to many a prayer, and zeal to many an effort, for the salvation of the noble-hearted Indian.[194]

---

194 "A Report from the Arkansas Gazette," *Baptist Missionary Magazine, 19* (March 1839), 64-65, reprinted from the Nashville, Tennessee, monthly, *The Baptist*. http://ualrexhibits.org/trailoftears/indian-removal/cherokee-removal-chronicle-1830-1839/

Daniel S. Butrick

Missionary

Starting Thursday, December 20, 1838

Thursday

As several waggons and some sick persons are still behind, we wait today for them. This morning a little child about 10 years old died. Previous to starting on this journey, I determined to let it be a journey of prayer, and to devote much time every day to that sacred duty, but instead of this. I have very strangely neglected prayer. In the morning our time is employed in taking our bed &tc, from the little waggon in which we sleep to the large waggon which carried its — replacing the seat. — getting water, — cooking breakfast, putting up things, harnessing &tc., soon we are hurried on by the waggons we accompany to the next encampment. Here we have to render what we did in the morning — put up our tent, get wood and water, prepare supper, fix our bed &ct. We often become much fatigued by the time we get our fire prepared. I know that all this cannot justify a neglect of prayer. I think my own heart is more peculiarly depraved, especially as respects impatient and angry feelings. And further, I have no pleasing anticipations about arriving at the Arkansas... The little boy who died last night was buried today in a coffin made of puncheons...

Saturday

This morning two children died with the bowel complaint. Towards night the wind arose and the air turning cold. I did not attend the prayer meeting...

Friday & Saturday

...It is disturbing to reflect on the situation of the nation. One detachment stopped at the Ohio River, two at the Mississippi, one four miles this side, one 16 miles this side, one 18 miles, and one 13 miles behind us. In all these detachments, comprising about 8,000 souls, there is now a vast amount of sickness, and many deaths. Six have died within a short time in Maj. Browns company, and in this detachment of Mr. Taylors there are more or less afflicted with sickness in almost every tent; and yet all are houseless & homeless in a strange land, and in a cold region, exposed to weather almost unknown in their native country. But they are prisoners. True their own chiefs have directly hold of their hands, yet the U. States officers hold the chiefs with an iron grasp, so that they are obliged to lead the people wording to their directions in executing effectually that Schermerhorn treaty.

Monday, Dec. 31.

...O what a year it has been! O what a sweeping wind has gone over, and carried its thousand into the grave; while thousands of others have been tortured and scarcely survive, and the whole nation comparatively thrown out of house & home during this most dreary winter. As coming from God, we know it is just. But what have they done to the U. States? Have they violated any treaty? or any intercourse law or abused any of the agents or officers of the U. States? or have they refused to accommodate U. States citizens when passing through the country? No such thing is pretended. For what crime then was this whole nation doomed to this perpetual death? This almost unheard of suffering? Simply because they would not agree to a principle which would be at once death to their national existence, viz.. that a few unauthorized individuals might, at any time, set aside the authority of the national council & principal chief, and in opposition to the declared will of the nation, dispose of the whole public domain, as well as the private property of individuals, and render the whole nation houseless and homeless at pleasure, such a treaty the President of the U. States sanctioned, the senate ratified, and the military force was found ready to execute. And now we see some of the effects.

The year past has also been a year of spiritual darkness. We have had but few happy seasons, and as for myself, I have by no means been faithful to my trust...

Tuesday Jan. 1, 1839.

Thus we enter on a new year in this wilderness, about 25 miles from the Mississippi. I say wilderness, because through many people are settled around us, yet we, Indians, have a little spot of wood land assigned us, in which we must reside as really as if all the region were a wilderness. White people come to sell & get gain, but not to invite any to a friendly roof.

...Though we have been distressed on every side, yet we have not been destroyed...

Monday.

Early this morning a blind man by the name of Avehy died with the bowel complaint. He had no family, but lived with two of his sisters. It is said they did not pay that attention to him, which his situation required. I had not known of his sickness, nor even heard of the man himself, till I heard of his death, though he has been all the time in the detachment. He was buried about dark near the tent where he died…

Monday, Jan. 14

A very aged Cherokee belonging to Mr. Wafford's detachment fell back into that of Mr. Taylors, the otherside of Ohio River, and crossed the river with us. One of our company … Little Broom broke his waggon and remained at Golconda a day or two and this old man remained with him. At length, however, the old man left him, & Little Broom came on. Soon after this Mr. Hicks detachment crossed the river & pursued his journey. Sometime after this the citizens near the river found the old man dead, and buried him. They then followed Mr. Hicks with a charge of 39 dollars for burying, though the corpse was hauled to the place of burying with a log chain & a yoke of oxen. Mr. Hicks told them the old man belonged to another detachment...

Tuesday.

We ... learn that last Friday night, a woman in the same company was killed by the fall of a tree, and two others wounded. The tree fell on them, it seems when asleep.[195]

195 Scerial Thompson, "The Cherokee Cross Egypt" *Journal of the Illinois State Historical Society (1908-1984) 44,* no. 4 (Winter, 1951): 289-304.

http://www.jstor.org/stable/40189170
http://www.illinoishistory.com/butrick.html

George Hicks

January 13, 1839

We done all in our power to remedy their destitute situation & contributed very much to their comfort by supplying them, so far as we could, with clothing Blankets & shoes, but still we have Suffered a great deal with sickness & have lost since the 21st of October last about 35, a great proportion of them were aged & children.[196]

196 Theda Perdue and Michael D. Green, *The Cherokee Removal: A Brief History with Documents* (Boston: Bedford / St. Martin's, 2005), 177.

A Report from the *Batesville News*

Smithville, Lawrence County, Arkansas

December 13, 1838

About twelve hundred Indians passed through this place yesterday, many of whom appeared very respectable. The whole company appear to be well clothed, and comfortably fixed for travelling. I am informed that they are very peaceable, and commit no depredations upon any property in the country through which they pass. They have upwards of one hundred wagons employed in transporting them; their horses are the finest I have ever seen in such a collection. The company consumes about one hundred and fifty bushels of corn per day.

It is stated that they have the measles and whooping-cough among them, and there is an average of four deaths per day."[197]

197 *Batesville News*, December 20, 1838 http://ualrexhibits.org/trailoftears/indian-removal/cherokee-removal-chronicle-1830-1839/

George Hicks and Collins McDonald

A letter to Chief John Ross

From Beatie's Prairie

March 15, 1839

Dear Sir,

We would respectfully inform you that we arrived here on yesterday the 14th Inst & that we are here and do not know what disposition to make of the public Teams & of the public property in our charge

We have no funds to pay for the Subsistence of the teams & the waggoners & we wish some immediate instructions on the subject

The Agent of the Government will be here today we will be mustered out of Service and Turned Over to government & we are informed that they have some shelled corn & Some very poor beef for our Subsistence which is unfit for use & from the promises made to us in the Nation East we did not Expect such treatment...

P.S. The people are in as good Health as could reasonably be Expected[198]

---

198 Charles River Editors, *The Trail of Tears: The Forced Removal of the Five Civilized Tribes* (Charles River Editors). 36. http://www.cherokee.org/AboutTheNation/History/TrailofTears/LetterfromJohnRoss.aspx

Martin Van Buren

US. President

Message to Congress

December, 1838

... It affords me sincere pleasure to apprise the Congress of the entire removal of the Cherokee Nation of Indians to their new homes west of the Mississippi. The measures authorized by Congress at its last session have had the happiest effect. By an agreement concluded with them by the commanding general in that country, their removal has been principally under the conduct of their own chiefs, and they have emigrated without any apparent reluctance.[199]

199 Edward Walker, *The Addresses and Messages of the Presidents of the United States, from Washington to Harrison* (Boston: Little and Brown, 1841), 658. http://www.presidency.ucsb.edu/ws/?pid=29480

A Native of Maine, Traveling in the Western Country

Special to the New York Observer

January 26, 1839

Some of the Cherokees are wealthy and travel in style. One lady passed on in her back in company with her husband, apparently with as much refinement and equipage as any of the mothers of New England; and she was a mother too and her youngest child, about three years old, was sick in her arms, and all she could do was to make it comfortable as circumstances would permit....She could only carry her dying child in her arms a few miles farther, and then she must stop in a stranger-land and consign her much loved babe to the cold ground, and that without pomp or ceremony, and pass on with the multitude...

When I past the last detachment of those suffering exiles and thought that my native countrymen had thus expelled them from their native soil and their much loved homes, and that too in this inclement season of the year in all their suffering, I turned from the sight with feelings which language cannot express and "wept like childhood then." I felt that I would not encounter the secret silent prayer of one of these sufferers armed with the energy that faith and hope would give it (if there be a God who avenges the wrongs of the injured) for all the lands of Georgia!

When I read in the President's Message that he was happy to inform the Senate that the Cherokees were peaceably and without reluctance removed — and remembered that it was on the third of December when not one of the detachments had reached their destination; and that a large majority had not made even half their journey when he made that declaration, I thought I wished the President could have been there that very day in Kentucky with myself, and have seen the comfort and the willingness with which the Cherokees were making their journey. But I forbear, full well I know that many prayers have gone up to the King of Heaven from Maine in behalf of the poor Cherokees.[200]

---

200 *New York Observer*, Jan. 26, 1839

Anonymous

Army and Navy Chronicle

Jan. 3, 1839

The Cherokees.–The steam boat Victoria arrived here on Saturday last, having on board 228 Cherokees, the last of the nation to be removed from the east of the Mississippi. They are mostly those who had been prevented by sickness from emigrating by land, with the main body of the nation. Some few are still scattered in the mountains of North Carolina, resisting all persuasions to join their brethren in their exodus from their fatherland. Among those on board the Victoria were John Ross and his family. Mr. Ross' wife, we regret to state, died shortly before reaching Little Rock, and was buried in the cemetery of this city.[201]

201 *Army and Navy Chronicle*, January 3, 1839. http://ualrexhibits.org/trailoftears/indian-removal/cherokee-removal-chronicle-1830-1839/

Anonymous

Arkansas Gazette

January 2, 1839

INDIAN MORTALITY. — Dr. Butler, one of the physicians of the emigrating Cherokees, computes that 2,000 out of 16,000, or one-eighth of the whole number, have died since they left their houses, and began to encamp for emigration in June last. — *New Orleans Bee*[202]

202 *Arkansas Gazette*, February 6, 1839

Anonymous

Batesville News

December 20, 1838

CHEROKEE INDIANS

On the 15th inst., a detachment of the Cherokee Indians passed near Batesville, Independence co., Ark., on their way to their new home in the "far west." Many of them came through the town to get their carriages repaired, horses shod, &c. &c.

The following are the principal officers among them: John Benge, Conductor; Geo. Lowry, Assistant, do.; Dr. W. P. Rawles, of Gallatin, Ten., Surgeon, and Physician; W. S. Coody, contractor.

They left Gunter's Landing, on Tennessee River, about 25 miles above Huntsville, Ala., the 10th of Oct.; since which time, owing to their exposure to the inclemency of the weather, and many of them being destitute of shoes, and other necessary articles of clothing, about 50 of them have died.

Doctor Rawles stands high in their estimation, as a friend to the Indians, and but few men are better qualified for the station he now occupies among them. He expects to accompany them all the way, and that he will not set out for home until about the 1st of January.

In the years of 1826-27, the writer of this brief notice labored among those Indians, as a Missionary; and truly, he found them to be an interesting people, ripe for the Gospel. He taught a mission school five days in the week, and preached on Saturdays and Sundays. Many were converted to the Christian faith, and for five months at a time, such was the exemplary piety of those who had professed religion, and such was the influence of the Gospel upon those who did not openly profess it, that he never saw a drunken man, nor heard an oath sworn, nor heard of a quarrel or fight in the neighborhood of the mission; neither did he ever hear the report of a gun, or an axe, during the above length of time, in the neighborhood, on the Sabbath day.

Several other missionaries, of different denominations, were laboring with and for them, in different parts of the Nation, at the same time.–Our success exceeded our most sanguine expectations. Thousands of them gave every necessary evidence of converting grace, and sometimes, scores professed religion at one meeting; and, unlike many others, they were not deterred by the distance of a few miles, from attending the preaching of the Gospel. If they could have regular preaching within ten or twelve miles of them, they felt that they were highly favored. Many times they were seen, from the hoary headed sire and matron, down to little boys and girls, wading through the mud and swamps for miles, to hear what the Great Spirit would say to them, through the instrumentality of the missionary.

Many large and flourishing societies and schools were gotten up among them. They had a Printing Press of their own, from which a weekly paper, called "The Cherokee Phoenix," was issued for some years, and edited by a native Cherokee. They also had the great part, if not the whole, of the New Testament translated into their own language. Indeed, no aboriginal tribe of Indians in North America, were tending faster toward civilization, and christianity, than the Cherokee.

But in the difficulties between them and the Georgians, and the General Government, the Georgians, I am credibly informed, destroyed their press; and the turbulence of the times had the unhappy tendency to break up their schools, dissolve their societies, and produce a state of general confusion and distress; so that many who had professed faith in Christ, measured back their steps to earth again. Many others, however, still hold on their way, and say, "they seek a home in heaven." May the Great Disposer of events overrule every thing for their good, and may they be prosperous and happy.

O Jesus the Cherokees save,

And bring them at last to thy rest;

And when they shall leave the cold grave,

May they then be found with the blest.[203]

---

203 *Batesville News*, December 20, 1838 http://ualrexhibits.org/trailoftears/indian-removal/cherokee-removal-chronicle-1830-1839/

Samuel Worcester

Missionary at New Echota

Relation of the events of June 22, 1839

Park Hill, Oklahoma

Mr. (Elias) Boudinot was yet living in my house. On Saturday morning, he went to his house, which he was building, a quarter of a mile distant. There some Cherokee men came up, inquiring for medicine, and Mr. Boudinot set out with two of them to come and get it. He had walked but a few rods, when his shriek was heard by his hired men, who ran to his help, but before they could come up the deed was done. A stab in the back with a knife, and seven gashes in the head with a hatchet, did the bloody work. He lived a few minutes, till we had time to arrive at the spot, and see him breathe his last — his wife among the rest — but he was speechless, and insensible to surrounding objects. The murderers ran a short distance into the woods, joined a company of armed men on horseback, and made their escape.[204]

---

204 Althea Bass, *Cherokee Messenger*, (Norman: University of Oklahoma Press, 1936), 255-256.

John Rollin Ridge

Relation of the events of June 22, 1839

In 1837, my father moved his family to his new home, he built his houses and opened his farm; gave encouragement to the riding neighborhood, and fed many a hungry and naked Indian whom oppression had prostrated, to the dust. A second time he built a schoolhouse, and Miss Sawyer again instructed his own children and the children of his neighbors. Two years culled away in quietude but the Spring of 1839 brought in a terrible train of events. Parties had arisen in the Nation. The removal West had fomented discontents of the darkest and deadliest nature. The ignorant Indians, unable to vent their rage on the whites, turned their wrath towards their own chiefs, and chose to hold them responsible for what had happened. John Ross made use of these prejudices to establish his own power. He held a secret council and plotted the death of my father and grandfather, and Boudinot, and others, who were friendly to the interests of these men. John Ridge was at the time the most powerful man in the Nation, and it was necessary for Ross, in order to realize his ambitious scheme for ruling the whole Nation, not only to put the Ridges out of the way, but those who most prominently supported them, lest they might cause trouble afterwards. These bloody deeds were perpetrated under circumstances of peculiar aggravation. On the morning of the 22nd of June, 1839, about day-break, our family was aroused from sleep by a violent noise. The doors were broken down, and the house was full of armed men. I saw my father in the hands of assassins. He endeavored to speak to them, but they shouted and drowned his voice, for they were instructed not to listen to him for a moment, for fear they would be persuaded not to kill him. They dragged him into the yard, and prepared to murder him. Two men held him by the arms, and others by the body, while another stabbed him deliberately with a dirk twenty-nine times. My mother rushed out to the door, but they pushed her back with their guns into the house, and prevented her egress until their act was finished, when they left the place quietly. My father fell to the earth, but did not immediately expire. My mother ran out to him. He raised himself on his elbow and tried to speak, but the blood flowed into his mouth and prevented him. In a few moments more he died, without speaking that last word which he wished to say. Then succeeded a scene of agony the sight of which might make one regret that the human race had ever been created. It has darkened my mind with an eternal shadow. In a room prepared for the purpose, lay pale in death the man whose voice had been listened to with awe and admiration in the councils of his Nation, and whose fame had passed to the remotest of the United States, the blood oozing through his winding sheet, and falling drop by drop on the floor. By his side sat my mother, with hands clasped, and in speechless agony — she who had given him her heart in the days of her youth and beauty, left the home of her parents, and followed the husband of her choice to a wild and distant land. And bending over him was his own afflicted mother, with her long, white hair flung loose over her shoulders and bosom, crying to the Great Spirit to sustain her in that dreadful hour. And in addition to all these, the wife, the mother and the little children, who scarcely knew their loss, were the dark faces of those who had been the murdered man's friends, and, possibly, some who had been privy to the assassination, who had come to smile over the scene.[205]

205 John Rollin Ridge, *Poems* (San Francisco: Edward Bosqui & Co., 1868), 6-8.

'Unhallowed Intrusion'

A headstone

Near the Conasauga River

On the road from Georgia to Tennessee

Sacred to the memory of David and Delilah A McNair, who departed this life, the former on the 15th of August, 1836, and the latter on the 30th of November, 1838. Their children, being members of the Cherokee Nation and having to go with their people to the West, do leave this monument, not only to show their regard for their parents, but to guard their sacred ashes against the unhallowed intrusion of the white man.[206]

---

206 See photo of gravesite on back cover.

Belle Kendrick Abbott

From the Atlanta Constitution

December 3, 1889

Perhaps the best forgotten historic spot in Georgia is New Echota, the once Indian capital of the nation, the place where the councils met and where the last treaty was made. It is now called New Town, though why entitled to this misnomer I cannot tell.

Upon inquiry as to where New Town was and what was there, I received only the unsatisfactory reply, 'It is four and a half miles from town, and there's nothin' left…'

...We had little trouble in finding the burying ground first. On the top of a slight elevation in the middle of a cottonfield plainly designated by the clump of dead and live chestnut trees, as well as hickories, which crowned the hill, we found it. They had cultivated up to the edge of the small burying ground, and through the cotton blooming freely in the mild September sunshine, I soon made my way. Parting the briars and underbrush there we found… a plain limestone slab at the head of a sunken, but grass-over-grown grave…

From the graveyard we found a winding road through horse lot gate, and corn fields to… the spot where the town was which once contained three hundred inhabitants. There was nothing to be seen but a most beautiful and blessed field of ripening corn, which covered many acres. Throughout this level sea of golden grain an occasional green walnut tree dotted the scene. These were indices, it seemed to me, that pointed to where human habitations once stood, and where human voices filled the air, instead of sighing, rustling corn.

At New Echota the Indians had their principal council house, where they met annually to transact the business of the nation. Their council consisted of a higher and a lower house, after the order of the Georgia legislature. This council house was a frame building, made after the fashion of the average country church, provided with benches for seats. Not a trace of the building remains. Up to these sessions of council the Indians came from all parts of the nation and remained in camp near by till the term was ended. It is said that when

John Ridge came home from school at the north he brought his father, Major Ridge, a fine carriage. And after this the major used to go to the council in great style, both riding and driving his favorite saddle horse, which was one of a fine pair hitched to the carriage. At New Echota the *Cherokee Phoenix* was printed, the first Cherokee paper ever published and was edited by Elias Boudinot. Here they also published Bibles and other books…

They had a blacksmith shop at New Echota, and the Indians did good and skillful work in that line, making hatchets, horseshoes, spikes, etc. Just beyond the town the Coosawattee and Conasauga comingle their waters and thus form the translucent, majestic Oostanaula which was a favorite river of the Cherokees. At the confluence of these two streams two Indians were shot in the water, by the United States troops, as they were trying to escape from their captivity at New Echota.

Upon inquiry as to what had become of the old 'block house' at New Echota, I was told that a Mr. Robert Prather had moved the logs from there several years ago, and had made him a corn crib out of them. I sought and found the corn crib as described. The logs seemed as sound as when cut from the forest. The little boy who held my parasol to keep off the burning sun as I sketched the crib, said to me innocently: 'Did the Injuns ever live in that crib?'

I have found since that this child knew about as much about that old block house, or anything else that once pertained to the Cherokees, as the average Georgian of much older years and broader research...[207]

207 Belle Kendrick Abbott, *Atlanta Constitution*, Dec. 3, 1889

Afterword

How many Cherokees died on the Trail of Tears? It's a question that gets asked a lot, but unfortunately there is no straightforward answer.

The most commonly quoted number is 4,000. Missionary Elizur Butler, who was a participant, suggested that number as early as 1839. [208] Anthropologist James Mooney, one of the most respected and renowned Cherokee scholars of the late nineteenth and early twentieth centuries, agreed that altogether "it is asserted, probably with reason, that over 4,000 Cherokee died as a direct result of the removal."[209]

Demographer Russell Thornton points out that this number "seems highly speculative," however. [210] "It appears to be only a suggested estimate, one without a hard factual basis, but one that subsequent scholars have cited and recited."

Anyone who has taken the Cherokee Nation history course (taught for many years by Julia Coates) knows that the numbers are controversial, even among tribal citizens.

"It was almost certainly not 4,000," Coates said during a course she taught in Rome, Georgia. She said that when you add up all the deaths noted by the various Cherokee-led detachments, you get 447 recorded deaths. About 500 died in the camps before the journey began, Coates said, "not 2,000, as has been asserted." If you also count those who died soon after arriving in the West, along with those who died earlier in the June, 1838 military-led detachments, you arrive at a number somewhere between 1,600 and 2,000, she said.

"That's still an eighth of the entire Cherokee population," said Coates.

"But there's almost a gut-level reaction. You want to hold onto that number of 4,000," she said. "Intuitively, you fear that people might say, 'Well, that's not that bad.' You think that the 4,000 number makes it seem more tragic, more horrific."

---

208 Thurman Wilkins, *Cherokee Tragedy: The Story of the Ridge Family and the Decimation of a People* (New York: The Macmillan Company, 1970) 315.

209 James Mooney, *History, Myths, and Sacred Formulas of the Cherokees* (Asheville: Bright Mountain Books, 1992), 133.

210 William L. Anderson, ed. *Cherokee Removal: Before and After*. (Athens: University of Georgia Press, 1991), 85.

But even the lower number has power, she said, when you realize that it consists mostly of small children and the elderly.

"Those under 10 years old were just lost," she said. "How strange would it feel if we lived in a society there were no children and no old people?" Many Cherokees lost all or most of their children in a span of just a few months, she said. "It's unimaginable," said Coates.

Add to that Thornton's assertion that "over 10,000 additional Cherokees would have been alive sometime during the period 1835 to 1840 had Cherokee removal not occurred,"[211] and one can see that numbers sometimes obscure as much as they reveal. Simple questions often do not have simple answers.

Was the tragedy any less for those who suffered on the Trail of Tears because probably only half as many died as has been commonly asserted?

"Some people are now looking at the numbers again and saying, 'Well, overall, the death rate really wasn't all that bad,'" said Coates.

"But I think they're really missing the point. We have a term for what happened here. It's called *ethnic cleansing*."

---

211 Ibid., 93.

Thus the State never intentionally confronts a man's sense, intellectual or moral, but only his body, his senses. It is not armed with superior wit or honesty, but with superior physical strength. I was not born to be forced. I will breathe after my own fashion. Let us see who is the strongest.

Henry David Thoreau

Civil Disobedience

1849

Appendix

B. B. Cannon

Conductor of a party of Emigrating Cherokee Indians

A Journal of Occurrences

Oct. 13th, 1837

Sent the waggons to the Indian encampment and commenced loading in the evening.

Oct. 14th 1837

Completed loading the waggons and crossed the Highwassie river at Calhoun, encamped at 5:00 P.M.

Oct. 15th, 1837

Marched the party at 8 O'C A.M. halted and encamped at Spring Creek at 11:0'C A.M. where Genl. Smith mustered the party, which consumed the remainder of the day. 5 miles to day.

Oct. 16th, 1837.

Marched at 8 o'c. A.M., halted and encamped at Kelly's ferry on Tennessee river, at 4 o'c. P.M. Issued corn & fodder, Corn meal & bacon, 14 miles to day.

Oct. 17th, 1837.

Commenced ferrying the Tennessee river at 8 o'c. A.M., having been detained until the sun dispelled the fog, every thing being in readiness to commence at day light, completed ferrying at 4 o'c. P.M. and reached little Richland creek at 8 o'c. P.M., where the Party had been directed to halt and encamp, Issued corn & fodder, 7 miles to day.

Oct. 18th, 1837.

Marched at 7 ½ o'c. A.M., one of the provision wagons oversat, detained a half hour, no damage done, ascended Wallens ridge, (the ascent 2 miles) halted at Ragsdale's at 1 ½ o'c. P.M., encamped and issued corn & fodder, corn-meal & bacon, 10 miles further to water, all wearied getting up the mountain, 5 miles today.

Oct. 19th, 1837.

Marched at 7 ½ o'c. A. M. descended the mountain, halted at 2 o'c. P.M., at Sequachee river near Mr. Springs, Issued corn & fodder, 11 ½ miles to day.

Oct. 20th, 1837.

Marched at 6 ½ o'c. A.M., ascended the Cumberland mountain, halted at Mr. Flemings, ¾ past 3 o'c. P.M., encamped and issued corn & fodder, corn meal & Bacon, 14 ½ miles to day.

Oct. 21st, 1837.

Marched at 7 ½ o'c. A.M., descended the mountain, halted at Collins river, 4 1/r o'c. P.M., encamped and issued corn & fodder, the Indians appear fatigued this evening. 13 miles today—road extremely rough.

Oct. 22nd, 1837.

Marched at 8 o'c. A.M. passed through McMinnville, halted at Mr. Britts ½ past 12 o'c. M., encamped and issued corn & fodder, corn meal & Bacon, Sugar and coffee to the waggoners & Interpreters, no water for 12 miles ahead, procured a quantity of corn meal and bacon to day. 7 ½ miles to day.

Oct. 23rd, 1837.

Marched at 6 ½ o'c. A.M., Capt. Prigmore badly hurt by a wagon horse attempting to run away, halted at Stone river near Woodbury, Te. ½ past 4 o'c. P.M., encamped and issued corn & fodder, 20 miles to day.

Oct. 24th, 1837.

Marched at 7 ½ o'c. A. M., halted at Mr. Yearwoods, 4 o'c. P.M., rained last night and to day, Issued corn & fodder, corn meal and bacon, 15 miles to day.

Oct. 25th, 1837.

Marched at 8 o'c. A.M., buried Andrew's child at ½ past 9 o'c. A.M., passed through Murfreesborough, halted at Overall's creek, 4 o'c. P.M., encamped and issued corn and fodder, 14 miles to day.

Oct. 26th, 1837.

Marched at 8 o'c. A.M., passed through three turnpike Gates, halted at Mr. Harris, 3 o'c. P.M., encamped and issued corn & fodder, corn meal & bacon, 16 ½ miles to day.

Oct. 27th, 1837.

Marched at 7 ½ o'c. A.M., passed through two Turnpike gates, and crossed the Cumberland river on the Nashville toll bridge, at Nashville, halted at Mr. Putnams ½ past 3 o'c. P.M., encamped and issued corn & fodder, Isaac Walker and emigrant belonging to the Party, overtook us. Mr. L. A. Kincannon, contracting agent, left us, and returned home, having, on the way, near McMinnville signified his intention, verbally, to do so, assigning as the reason the delicate situation of his health, 13 miles to day.

Oct. 28th, 1837.

Rested for the purpose of washing clothes, repairing wagons, and shoeing horses. Reese, Starr and others of the emigrants visited Genl. Jackson who was at Nashville, Issued corn & fodder, corn-meal and bacon, Assigned Mr. E. S. Curry to supply the place of Mr. Kincannon.

Oct. 29th, 1837.

Marched at 8 ½ o'c. A.M., halted at Long creek ½ past 2 o'c. P.M., encamped and issued corn & fodder, 13 ½ miles to day.

Oct. 30th, 1837.

Marched at 7 ½ o'c A.M., halted at Little red river ½ past 5 o'c. P.M., encamped and issued corn & fodder, corn-meal & Bacon, 18 ½ miles to day.

Oct. 31st, 1837.

Marched at 8 o'c. A.M., halted at Graves, Ken. 3 o'c. P.M.,Issued corn & fodder, 16 miles to day.

Nov. 1st, 1837.

Marched at 8 o'c., A.M., buried Ducks child, passed throug Hopkinsville, Ken, halted at Mr. Northerns ½ past 5 o'c. P.M.

Encamped & issued corn & fodder, Flour and bacon, 19 miles to day.

Nov. 2nd, 1837.

Marched at 8 o'c. A.M. and halted one mile in advance of Mr.Mitchersons, 3 o'o. P.M., encamped and issued corn and fodder.

Nov. 3rd, 1837.

David Timpson and Pheasant, emigrants belonging to the party, came up last night in the stage, having been heretofore enrolled, and mustered, marched at 8 o'c. A.M., passed thro' Princeton, Ken., halted and encamped near Mr. Barnetts, at ½ past 4 o'c. P.M.

Issued corn & fodder, Flour & bacon, 17 miles to day.

Nov. 4th, 1837.

Marched at 8 o'c. A.M., halted and encamped at Threlkelds branch, 4 o'c, P.M., Issued corn & fodder, 15 miles to day.

Nov. 5th, 1837.

Marched at 8 o'c. A.M., passed thro' Salem, Ken., halted and encamped at another Mr. Threlkelds branch at 4 o'c. P.M., Issued corn & fodder, corn meal, a small quantity of flour, and bacon, 13 ½ miles to day.

Nov. 6th, 1837.

Marched at 7 o'c. A.M., arrived at Berry's ferry (Golconda opposite on the Ohio river) 9 o'c. A.M., every thing in readiness to commence ferrying, but Prevented on account of the extreme high winds and consequent roughness of the river, which continued the remainder of the day, encamped in the evening, Issued corn & fodder, 5 ½ miles to day.

Nov. 7th, 1837.

Commenced ferrying at ½ past 5 o'c. A.M., moved the Party as it crossed one mile out and encamped. Completed crossing 4 o'c. P.M., all safely, Issued corn & fodder, corn meal & bacon, 1 mile to day.

Nov. 8th, 1837.

Marched at 8 o'c. A.M., Mr. Reese & myself remained behind, and buried a child of Seabolts, overtook the Party, halted and encamped at Big Bay creek, 4 o'c. P.M., Issued corn & fodder, (James Starr & wife, left this morning with two carry-alls to take care of, and bring on three of their children, who were too sick to travel—with instructions to overtake the Party as soon as possible without endangering the lives of their children.)—15 miles to day.

Nov. 9th, 1837.

Marched at 8 o'c., A.M., halted and encamped at Cash creek, ½ past 4 o'c. P.M., Issued corn & fodder, corn meal & Bacon, 15 miles to day.

Nov. 10th, 1837.

Marched at 8 o'c. A.M., were detained 2 hours on the way making a bridge across a small creek, halted at Cypress creek, 4 o'c., P.M., encamped and issued corn & fodder, & salt, 14 miles to day.

Nov. 11th, 1837.

Marched at 8 o'c, A.M., passed thro' Jonesboro' Ill., halted and encamped at Clear creek, in the Mississippi river bottom, ½ past 3 o'c. P. M., Issued corn & fodder, corn meal & bacon—13 miles to day, issued sugar & coffee to the wagoners, & interpreters.

Nov. 12th, 1837.

Marched at 8 o'c. A.M., arrived at Mississippi river, 10 o'c. A.M., Commenced ferrying, at 11 o'c. A. M., directed the party to move a short distance as they crossed the river, and encamp, Issued corn & fodder, Starr came up, the health of his children but little better, Richard Timberlake and George Ross, overtook us and enrolled, attached themselves to Starrs family.

Nov. 13th, 1837.

Continued ferrying from 7 o'c. until 10 o'c. A.M., when the wind arose and checked our progress, 3 o'c. P.M., resumed and made our trip, suspended at 5 o'c. P.M., Issued corn & fodder, corn meal & bacon, buried another of Duck's children to day.

Nov. 14th, 1837.

Crossed the residue of the Party, Marched at 10 o'c. A. M., halted and encamped at Mr. William's, Issued corn & fodder, sickness prevailing, 5 miles to day.

Nov. 15th, 1837.

Rested for the purpose of washing &c., Issued corn and fodder, corn meal and bacon.

Nov. 16th, 1837.

Marched at 8 o'c. A. M., left Reese, Starr and families on account of sickness in their families, also James Taylor (Reese's son in law) and family, Taylor himself being very sick, with instructions to overtake the Party, passed thro' Jackson, Mo., halted & encamped at widow Roberts on the road via Farmington &c., Issued corn only, no fodder to be had, 17 miles to day.

Nov. 17th, 1837.

Marched at 8 o'c. A. M., halted at White Water creek 4 o'c. P.M., Issued corn & fodder, corn meal and beef, 13 miles to day.

Nov. 18th, 1837.

Marched at 8 o'c. A.M., halted and encamped at Mr. Morand's 5 o'c. P.M., Issued corn & fodder, Flour & bacon, 16 miles to day.

Nov. 19th, 1837.

Marched at 8 o'c. A.M., halted and encamped ½ past 4 o'c. P.M., at Wolf creek, Issued corn & fodder, 14 miles to day.

Nov. 20th, 1837.

Marched at 8 o'c. A.M., passed thro' Farmington, Mo., halted at St. Francis river, 4 o'c. P.M., encamped and issued corn & fodder, Flour & beef, 15 miles to day.

Nov. 21st, 1837.

A considerable number drunk last night obtained the liquor at Farmington yesterday, had to get out of bed about midnight to quell the disorder, a refusal by several to march this morning, alledging that they would wait for Starr & Reese to come up at that place, Marched at 8 o'c., A. M. in defiance of threats and attempts to intimidate, none remained behind, passed through Caledonia, halted at Mr. Jacksons, encamped and issued corn & fodder, beef and Bacon, mostly bacon, 14 miles to day.

Nov. 22nd 1837.

Marched 8 ½ o'c. A.M., pass through the lead mines (or Courtois diggings), halted at Scotts, 4 o'c. P.M., issued corn, fodder, and corn meal, 13 miles to day.

Nov. 23rd, 1837.

Rested for the purpose of repairing wagons, shoeing horses, washing &c., Starr, Reese, and Taylor came up, the health of their families in some degree improved, Issued corn & fodder, and beef, weather very cold.

Nov. 24th, 1837.

Marched at 8 ½ o'c. A.M., Considerable sickness prevailing, halted at Huzza creek, 4 o'c. P.M., encamped and issued corn & fodder, 12 miles to day.

Nov. 25th, 1837.

Doct. Townsend, officially advised a suspension of our march, in consequence of the severe indisposition of several families, for a time sufficient for the employment of such remedial agents as their respective cases might require. I accordingly directed the Party to remain in camp and make the best possible arrangement for the sick, In the evening issued corn & fodder, flour and beef.

Nov. 26th, 1837.

Remained in camp, sickness continuing and increasing, Issued corn & fodder, beef & corn meal.

Nov. 27th, 1837.

Remained in camp, sickness continuing to increase, Issued corn & fodder, Bacon & corn meal.

Nov. 28th, 1837.

Moved the Detachment two miles further to a Spring and School-house, obtained permission for as many of the sick to occupy the school-house as could do so, a much better situation for an encampment than on the creek, sickness increasing, Issued corn & fodder.

Nov. 29th, 1837.

Remained in camp, sickness still increasing, buried Corn Tassels child to day, Issued corn & fodder.

Nov. 30th, 1837.

Remained in camp, sickness continuing, Issued corn and fodder.

December 1st, 1837.

Remained in camp, sickness abating, Issued cor and fodder, Bacon & corn meal, Buried Oolanheta's child to day.

Decr. 2nd, 1837.

Remained in camp, sickness abating, Issued corn & fodder, Beef & corn meal.

Decr. 3rd, 1837.

Remained in camp, sickness abating, Issued corn & fodder.

Decr. 4th, 1837.

Marched at 9 o'c. A.M., Buried George Killian, and left Mr. Wells to bury a waggoner, (black boy) who died this morning, scarcely room in the wagons for the sick, halted at Mr. Davis, 12 past 4 o.c. P.M., had to move down the creek a mile off the road, to get wood, Issued corn & fodder and corn meal, 11 miles to day.

Decr. 5th, 1837.

Marched 9 o'c. A.M., left two waggoners (black boys) at Mr. Davis sick, this morning, halted at the Merrimack river, ½ past 3 o'c. P.M., Encamped and issued corn and fodder, corn meal and beef, 10 miles to day.

Decr. 6th, 1837.

Marched at 9 o'c. A.M., passed Masseys Iron works, halted at Mr. Jones' ½ past 3 o'c. P. M., encamped and issued corn and fodder, 12 miles to day.

Decr. 7th, 1837.

Marched at 8 ½ o'c., A.M., Reese's team ran away, broke his wagon and Starrs carry-all, left him and family to get his wagon mended, at 17 miles, and to overtake if possible, halted at Mr. Bates son, 5 o'c., P.M., encamped and issued corn and fodder, corn-meal & bacon, 20 miles to day.

Decr. 8th, 1837.

Buried Nancy Bigbears Grand Child, marched at 9 o'c. A.M., halted at Piney a small river, ½ past 3 o'c. P.M., rained all day, encamped and issued corn only, no fodder to be had, several drunk, 11 miles to day.

December the 9th, 1837.

Marched at 9 o'c. A.M., Mayfields wagon broke down at about a mile left him to get it mended and overtake, halted at Waynesville, Mo. 4 o'c. P.M., encamped and issued corn & fodder, beef & corn meal, weather extremely cold, 12 ½ miles to day.

Decr. 10th, 1837.

Marched at 8 o'c. A.M., halted at the Gasconade river 4 o'c. P.M., Issued corn & fodder. 14 miles to day.

Decr. 11th, 1837.

Marched at ½ past 8 o'c. A. M., halted at Sumner's 4 o'c. P.M., encamped and issued corn & fodder. 15 miles to day.

Decr. 12th, 1837.

Marched at 9 o'c. A.M., halted one mile in advance of Mr. Parkes at a branch, 4 o'c. P. M., encamped and issued corn & fodder, corn meal, beef and a small quantity of bacon. 14 miles to day.

Decr. 13th, 1837.

Marched at 8 ½ o'c. A. M., halted at a branch near Mr. Eddington's, 4 o'c. P.M., encamped and issued corn & fodder, Reese & Mayfield came up, 13 ½ miles today.

Decr. 14th, 1837.

Marched at 8 o'c. A. M., halted at James fork of White river, near the road but which [p. 13] does not cross the road, 3 o'c. P. M., Mr. Wells taken sick, Issued corn meal, corn & fodder, 15 ½ miles to day.

Decr. 15th, 1837.

Joseph Starrs wife had a child last night. Marched at 8 ½ o'c. A. M., halted at Mr. Danforths, 1 ½ P. M., waggoners having horses shod until late at night, encamped & issued corn & fodder & beef. 10 ½ miles to day.

Decr. 16th, 1837.

Issued sugar & coffee to the waggoners & Interpreters this morning, Marched at 9 o'c. A. M., passed through Springfield Mo., halted at Mr. Clicks, 4 o'c. P. M., encamped and issued corn & fodder and corn-meal. 12 miles to day. (left Mr. Wells)

Decr. 17th, 1837.

Snowed last night, Buried Eleges wife and Chas. Timberlakes son (Smoker), Marched at 9 o'c. A. M., halted at Mr. Dyes 3 o'c P.M., extremely cold weather, sickness prevailing to a considerable extent, all very much fatigued, encamped and issued corn & fodder, & beef. 10 miles to day.

Decr. 18th, 1837.

Detained on account of sickness, Doct. Townsend sent back to Springfield for medicines, buried Dreadful Waters this evening, Issued corn and fodder & corn meal.

Decr. 19th, 1837.

Detained to day also on account of sickness, cold intense, Issued corn & fodder and beef.

Decr. 20th, 1837.

Marched at 8 ½ o'c. A. M., halted at Mr. Allens ½ past 3 o'c. P. M., encamped, and issued corn & fodder & corn meal. 15 miles to day.

Decr. 21st, 1837.

Marched at 8 o'c. A. M., halted at Lockes on Flat creek, 12 past 3 o'c. P. M., encamped and issued corn & fodder, & beef. 15 miles to day.

Decr. 22nd, 1837.

Buried Goddards Grand child, Marched at 8 o'c. A. M., halted at McMurtrees, 3 o'c. P.M., encamped and issued corn & fodder and corn-meal. 15 miles to day.

Decr. 23rd, 1837.

Buried Rainfrogs daughter (Lucy Redstick's child). Marched at 8 o'c. A. M. halted at Reddix, 3 o'c. P. M., encamped and issued corn & fodder & beef. 16 miles to day.

Decr. 24th, 1837.

Marched at 8 o'c. A. M., halted at the X hollows, had to leave the road ¾ of a mile to get water, 3 o'c. P. M., Issued corn & fodder, Pork and corn meal. 15 miles to day.

Decr. 25th, 1837.

Marched at 8 o'c. A. M., took the right hand [p. 15] road to Cane hill, at Fitzgeralds, halted a half mile in advance of Mr.

Cunninghams at a branch, 3 o'c. P. M., Issued corn & fodder and salt Pork. 15 ½ miles to day.

Decr. 26th, 1837.

Marched at 8 o'c. A.M., halted at James Coulters on Cane hill, Ark. ½ past 3 o'c P. M., encamped and issued corn meal, corn & fodder, 16 ½ miles to day.

Decr. 27th, 1837.

Buried Alsey Timberlake, Daughter of Chas Timberlake, Marched at 8 o'c. A. M., halted at Mr. Beans, in the Cherokee nation west, at ½ past 2 o'c. P. M., encamped and issued corn & fodder, Fresh pork & some beef. 12 miles to day.

Decr. 28th, 1837.

The Party refused to go further, but at the same time pledged themselves to remain together until the remuster was made by the proper officer, for whom I immediately sent an express to Fort Gibson, they alleged at the same time that the refusal was in consequence of the sickness now prevailing and that only.

Doct. Reynolds Disbursing agent for the Party dismissed the wagons from further service, Buried another child of Chas Timberlakes, and one which was born (untimely) yesterday of which no other account than this is taken, Jesse Half Breeds wife had a child last night, issued Pork, corn meal and flour, corn & fodder for today.

Lieut. Van Horne arrived late this evening, having missed the express on the way.

Decr. 29th, 1837.

Remustered the Party, Issued a small quantity of corn meal & Pork yet on hand.

Decr. 30th, 1837.

Completed the Rolls of Remuster, turned over the Party to Lieut. Van Horne, and dismissed my assistants.[212]

---

212 "An Overland Journey to the West" (October-December 1837) by B. B. Cannon Oct.-Dec. 1837, pp. 36-43, "The Removal of the Cherokee," *Journal of Cherokee Studies*. http://ualrexhibits.org/trailoftears/eyewitness-accounts/journal-of-bb-cannon-cherokee-removal-1837/

Bibliography

Anderson, William L., ed. *Cherokee Removal: Before and After.* (Athens: University of Georgia Press, 1991).

Various historians examine the causes of the Cherokee Removal.

Boulware, Tyler. *Deconstructing the Cherokee Nation: Town, Region, and Nation among Eighteenth Century Cherokees.* (Gainesville: University Press of Florida, 2011).

Boulware argues for the importance of the concept of "town" in the formation of Cherokee identity and agency during the late eighteenth and early nineteenth centuries.

Brown, John P. *Old Frontiers.* (Kingsport: Southern Publishers, 1938).

Brown, a Tennessee historian who was well-versed in primary source material as well as local lore and traditional stories, writes one of the earliest narrative histories of the Cherokee removal and the events leading up to it, focusing especially on the guerilla warfare tactics of the Chickamauga Cherokees who lived in the Lookout Mountain area.

Burnett, John G. "The Cherokee Removal Through the Eyes of a Private Soldier." *Journal of Cherokee Studies* 3, no. 3 (1978): 50-55.

A Removal-era soldier recounts the Trail of Tears in what he described as a first-person account.

Conley, Robert J. *The Cherokee Nation, a History.* (Albuquerque: University of New Mexico Press, 2005).

The only history of the Cherokee Nation commissioned by the tribe, written by a tribal citizen.

Debo, Angie. *And Still the Waters Run: The Betrayal of the Five Civilized Tribes.* (Princeton: Princeton University Press, 1972).

A widely recognized, influential, and commonly cited work, first published in 1940, outlining the causes of Indian removal.

Ehle, John. *Trail of Tears: The Rise and Fall of the Cherokee Nation.* (New York: Anchor Books, 1988).

A popular history aimed at a wide audience, utilizing curated snippets of primary source documents to weave an engaging tale of the events leading up to the Trail of Tears.

Foreman, Grant. *Indian Removal.* (Norman: University of Oklahoma Press, 1972).

First published in 1932, this has long been considered one of the definitive historical examinations of Indian removal.

Foreman, Grant. *The Five Civilized Tribes: Cherokee, Chickasaw, Choctaw, Creek, Seminole*. Norman: University of Oklahoma Press, 1971.

An influential early work on the Trail of Tears, and now a standard text.

Hill, Sarah H. "To Overawe the Indians and Give Confidence to the Whites: Preparations for the Removal of the Cherokee Nation from Georgia." *Georgia Historical Quarterly* 95, no. 4 (2011): 465-497.

Hill argues that fear and resentment shaped the methods of removal of the Cherokees in 1838. Even though Cherokees were generally peaceful, ignorant soldiers often engaged in unlawful conduct.

Hill, Sarah. *Weaving New Worlds: Southeastern Cherokee Women and their Basketry.* (Chapel Hill: University of North Carolina Press, 1997).

Hill colorfully describes the ancient art of basket weaving within a larger cultural and anthropological context.

Hobgood, Ronald. "The First Tears of the Trail: Archaeological Investigations of Potential Cherokee Removal Fort Sites in Georgia." *Early Georgia* 37, no. 1 (2009):101-131.

Hobgood investigates a number of possible fort and camp sites used by the military during the removal of the Cherokee Indians in 1838. Sites he investigates include Fort Cumming in LaFayette, Fort Hoskins in Spring Place, and Fort Hetzel in Ellijay. He concludes that the Hetzel and Cumming sites have suffered from too many adverse impacts from local development to be productive for any further study. The Fort Hoskins site, however, yield a number of nineteenth century artifacts.

King, Duane. *The Cherokee Trail of Tears* (Portland: Graphic Arts Books, 2007).

A brief overview of detachments that traveled the Trail of Tears and the various routes they took.

Lewis, Thomas and Madeline Kneberg, *Tribes that Slumber:*

Indians of the Tennessee Region (Knoxville: University of Tennessee Press, 1986).

The authors describe field work undertaken by the Smithsonian Institute during the mid- twentieth century.

Malone, Henry Thompson. *Cherokees of the Old South.* (Athens: University of Georgia Press, 1956).

The author concentrates much of his focus on prominent Georgia Cherokees such as Stand Watie, Major Ridge, and Elias Boudinot, arguing that Cherokee history is best understood as a conflict between these more affluent and educated "mixed blood" Cherokees against the traditionalists, led by Chief John Ross and others.

McLoughlin, William G. *Cherokee Renascence in the New Republic.* (Princeton: Princeton University Press, 1986).

The author examines how the "civilization" policies of the early American republic influenced the development of the Cherokee Nation.

McLoughlin, William G. *Cherokees and Missionaries, 1789-1839.* New Haven: Yale University Press, 1984.

The author looks at the role missionaries played in the acculturation of the Cherokees.

McLoughlin, William G. "Georgia's Role in Instigating Compulsory Indian Removal." *Georgia Historical Quarterly* 70, no. 4 (1986):605-632.

McLoughlin tries to decipher what motivated the Georgians to remove the Cherokee Indians from the state. The main cause of removal, he says, was the "rise of romantic nationalism" and intertwined ideas of state's rights. He also argues that Georgia originally intended to make amends for the Yazoo fraud, and that its leaders "misread" the state's Compact of 1802 with the federal government. He argues that the Indians also played a role in their removal as they took sides against the Americans in several conflicts.

Miles, Tiya. *The House on Diamond Hill: A Cherokee Plantation Story.* (Chapel Hill: The University of North Carolina Press, 2012).

Miles, a MacArthur Foundation grant recipient, explores the romanticized, largely obscured plantation past of the Chief Vann House, a state historic site in Chatsworth.

Miles, Tiya. *Ties that Bind: The Story of an Afro-Cherokee Family in Slavery and Freedom.* (Berkeley: University of California Press, 2006).

A microhistory that explores complex race and gender relations in the early Cherokee Nation.

Mooney, James. Myths *of the Cherokees and Sacred Formulas of the Cherokees.* (Nashville: Charles Elder, 1972).

A seminal work on the history and mythology of the Eastern Band of Cherokee Indians, written by an early Smithsonian anthropologist.

Perdue, Theda. *Cherokee Women.* Lincoln: University of Nebraska Press, 1999.

An oft-cited work on the complex matrilineal society of the Cherokees.

Perdue, Theda. *Slavery and the Evolution of Cherokee Society.* (Knoxville: University of Tennessee Press, 1979).

An examination of race and slavery in the Cherokee Nation of the late eighteenth and early nineteen centuries.

Perdue, Theda and Michael Green. *The Cherokee Nation and the Trail of Tears.* (New York: Penguin Books, 2008).

The authors detail the betrayals of the United States government against the Cherokee Nation and the hardships endured by the Cherokee people.

Royce, Charles C. *The Cherokee Nation of Indians.* (Chicago: Aldine Publishing Company, 1975).

One of the earliest histories of the Cherokee Nation.

Smith, Gordon Burns. *History of the Georgia Militia 1783-1861.* (Milledgeville: Boyd Publishing, 2000).

An overview of the Georgia militia, which was engaged in the removal of the Cherokees from their homelands in the Southeast in 1938.

Starr, Emmet. *History of the Cherokee Indians and their Legends and Folk Lore.* (Norman: University of Oklahoma Press, 1968).

This work is considered by many Cherokee Nation citizens to be the definitive history and genealogy of the tribe.

Thornton, Russell. *The Cherokees: A Population History.* Lincoln: University of Nebraska Press, 1990.

Thornton looks at the population levels of the Cherokee

tribe over the course of the last three centuries and draws conclusions about the impacts their interactions with whites had on their society, both positive and negative.

Walker, Robert Sparks. *Torchlights to the Cherokees: The Brainerd Mission.* (Johnson City: Overmountain Press, 1993).

Sparks details the daily life and interactions of Christian missionaries living in the Cherokee Nation in what is now the Chattanooga, Tennessee area.

Williams, David. *The Cherokee Gold Rush: Twenty-Niners, Cherokees, and Gold Fever.* (Columbia: University of South Carolina Press, 1993).

A brief account of the Georgia gold rush, a widely recognized contributing factor leading to the Cherokee removal.

Woodward, Grace Steele. *The Cherokees.* (Norman: University of Oklahoma Press, 1963).

An overview of Cherokee history for a popular audience.

Online sources:

https://southernspaces.org/2017/all-roads-led-rome-facing-history-cherokee-expulsion.

https://southernspaces.org/2012/cherokee-removal-scenes-ellijay-georgia-1838.

http://www.nps.gov/trte/historyculture/upload/Georgia-Forts.pdf .

http://www.wcu.edu/library/DigitalCollections/CherokeePhoenix/Vol3/no18/3no18_p2-c5A.htm.

W. Jeff Bishop served for many years as president of the Georgia chapter of the Trail of Tears Association, heading up National Park Service-funded research projects investigating Cherokee Removal fort site archaeology and the history of the Chief John Ross House and Running Waters Council Ground. He also developed the Georgia Trail of Tears National Historic Trail brochure. He has a master's degree in public history and certification in museum studies from the University of West Georgia and currently serves on the Friends of New Echota board of directors. He was recently appointed by the governor to serve on the Georgia Historical Records Advisory Council. He serves as executive director of the Newnan-Coweta Historical Society and lives with his wife and five children in Newnan, Georgia.

Printed in the USA
CPSIA information can be obtained
at www.ICGtesting.com
LVHW090222101123
763529LV00002B/150

9 780988 956872